# FROM HAND TO HOME

# FROM HAND TO HOME

## THE ARCHITECTURE OF DOUGLAS WRIGHT

### BY DOUGLAS WRIGHT

WRITTEN WITH JUDITH NASATIR
FOREWORD BY BUNNY WILLIAMS AND
BRIAN J. McCARTHY

New York Paris London Milan

# CONTENTS

Foreword 6  Introduction 8  **PLACE** 14  Houses 18  Summer Retreat 22  Water's Edge 36  Beachside Modern 56  A New Look 78  By the Bay 102  River's Edge 122  Suburban Pavilion 146  Forest to Field 158  **INSPIRATION** 174  Apartments 178  **THE HAND** 244  The Future 248  Floor and Site Plans 250  Acknowledgments 254  Credits 256

# FOREWORD
## A CONVERSATION WITH BUNNY WILLIAMS AND BRIAN McCARTHY

**BUNNY WILLIAMS, BRIAN McCARTHY,** and **DOUGLAS WRIGHT** share a history at Parish-Hadley, a storied powerhouse of design, decoration, and architecture. In the following conversation, Williams and McCarthy discuss the evolution of that legacy in Wright's architecture today.

**BUNNY WILLIAMS:** The awareness of form meeting function to create comfort is part of the incredible education that sets apart all architects who came from Parish-Hadley. Doug makes beautiful exteriors, but he knows that houses are meant to be lived in. As he works on the facades of a house, he is constantly thinking about the interior architecture, too: that rooms function for their purpose, that windows are correctly placed, that there is space for furniture.

**BRIAN McCARTHY:** Before we see the plans for the first time, Doug is already considering where to put furniture, which is, again, part of our shared foundation from Parish-Hadley. To be in a design studio with Albert Hadley constantly coming in, looking over your shoulder, and talking about how he was imagining the rooms was so special. He would sketch as you sat with him, which was very helpful for everyone involved in the project but so rare. Doug also loves to do that, and when he starts doodling, it becomes its own language.

**BW:** Albert taught us that even if you cannot really draw, if you can sketch out a room in your mind's eye and imagine how to place the furniture, when you ultimately put it on paper, it is more than a floor plan. You are able to build up all the elevations and determine what each wall will be. Doug does this beautifully. And because we—interior designer and architect—have thought through each space together from the outset, we end up with easy-to-furnish rooms that function beautifully for their designated use.

**BM:** Doug is also so open to the kind of discussion that leads to the best possible results. He wants to be pushed to think outside the box, and he pushes us to do the same.

**BW:** Albert always taught us to look ahead, to think, to dream, and to imagine in a more contemporary way even though we were based in tradition. Doug exemplifies this. He is equally comfortable working in traditional and modern styles. His contemporary architecture, though, has the rich classical background that comes from a thorough consideration of design, proportion, and scale.

**BM:** Albert and Mrs. Parish inspired all of us to explore, to be curious, to keep our minds and eyes open, to continue to learn, and to think differently. Doug has been on a grand tour for the past thirty-five years with his travels and education, the firms he has worked with, developing his own firm, and now mentoring the people in his office. His work has a definite twenty-first-century flair. He is clearly thinking about tomorrow, not yesterday.

**BW:** It is so important to constantly look at new things and be receptive to novel ideas. But it is just as critical to know and understand the fundamentals, such as the idea of rooms. Some people prefer wide-open loft spaces, but the average person wants at least a degree of separation. What makes spaces distinct from one another when the design is contemporary and there are no trims, obvious definitions, and thresholds? Doug has absorbed the language of traditional backgrounds over the years so he can treat the elements in a fresh way without losing the reality of how houses actually work.

**BM:** The spatial sequence is a basic, foundational principle of design, and it applies to everything we do, traditional or modern. Doug understands this.

**BW:** It sounds old-fashioned to talk about function. But it is so important for an architect to understand that a house needs to operate smoothly to be comfortable, and that areas like the laundry room and back-of-house spaces can make it or break it in this regard. Doug's training makes this automatic.

**BM:** Matters of functionality always come first, even before envisioning a project's beauty or style. Asking clients probing questions up front about how they want to live is essential, not least because these questions encourage clients to analyze carefully what their needs really are. Doug is excellent at checking all these boxes from the start.

**BW:** Great projects also always involve the three design disciplines: architecture, interior design, and landscape. Doug respects and enjoys teamwork, and for him the collaboration is as exciting as designing the house or the apartment.

**BM:** Each project is not just about what you see within the room—it is what you see beyond the room, and from the outside looking in. This was how we worked every day at Parish-Hadley, and it is second nature to us and Doug because of that wonderful education.

**BW:** As you begin to see Doug's process in this book, you realize that he addresses every single detail, with incredible atmosphere. His architecture is beautifully designed, and it has a soul, a flavor, that his drawings, sketches, and watercolors reveal.

**BM:** Doug's love of drawing and painting reflects the artistry behind the architect shown in these pages. His watercolors also inform him, and us, of so many details, nuances, and play with light. He lives with his eyes wide open. What better way to go through life?

# INTRODUCTION

I have always loved architecture, in part because the learning never stops. It is a field of pursuit, study, and practice where history is palpably present. The treasury of architectural precedents is in front of us every day, and there is always so much more to discover and understand. So much of life in general as well as acquired wisdom plays a role in creating and constructing anything of lasting merit. What we build is inextricably of our time, and in that way modern, whether it looks so or wears a traditional guise. We cannot help but be connected to the architectural continuum. For me, the marriage of the classical and the modern makes everything I design a hybrid, an amalgam of influences—so often about classic space-making, but also dramatically knowing, seeing, and bringing out the modern intent and openness within.

What I admire most about classical architecture is its underlying idea of order and how that emphasis on organization, hierarchy, progression, and precision shapes the way our experience of place unfolds. This feeling of place is a large part of what I try to capture in every house, in every project I design.

Wherever we have learned the language of architecture, whoever our mentors, whatever our influences and traditions, the questions in placemaking remain the same: What do we see along the road as we head to the site? What is the panorama that unfolds down the driveway or entry road? At the front door? When the door opens? How do we progress/process from the entry through the front hall to the main living room and beyond? The same holds for a club or institutional building. So much of how we live now responds in one way or another to this concept of the choreographed reveal, of the consciously planned procession of introduction, whether intuited or imposed. This is just as true of the most classical design as it is of a glass box that alights in a landscape.

Every project, therefore, becomes a distillation of existing ideas, of my ongoing education and evolving connection with the world. Travel and study add richness to the education I bring to bear, and that serves as support through the problem-solving process that is design. The tension between the traditional and the modern, the old and the new, can be so productive. My goal is to find harmony and beauty within the certain motifs of living that are germane to each project and marry that to the best solution for the specific client and their needs and desires.

As I get to know my clients, what excites them, what their hopes, preferences, needs, and dreams are, the spark of understanding, an inkling of what would be an appropriate

architecture, begins to emerge. The nature of the place itself and its unique physical aspects inevitably factors into the equation. Is the property on the coast? In the forest? On a hillside? In getting to know all these different facets—light, shade, and vistas, artistic interests, desires, the scents of the site and gardens, the experience of progression from one hundred miles away to the destination itself—a set of qualities comes to the fore to inform my understanding of the place and its identity. The challenge is always to carry this perception and concept of the large scale through to the intimate. The notion is really one of building a metaphor.

I love listening to how my clients want to live because I hear the architecture in their responses. Someone might express his or her joy at feeling a sense of surprise walking through the front door, or marvel at a wash of sunlight, or the wonder of luxuriating in complex shaded and sunlit spaces, or the comfort that visible connections to the surroundings brings. These comparatively simple asks allow for enormous design leeway. So often my design solutions come about through the client's stories, perhaps of childhood summers spent in the mountains, of hiking the forests and the fields, or of a lifetime of memories tied to the family homestead.

As a kid, I drew all the time, built models, and constructed insane sandcastles every summer at the beach. My father collected books on architecture, on houses and the great estates and palaces of Europe, and elsewhere around the world, so I was always looking and absorbing. Our house in Pennsylvania was a traditional, well-designed American house from the 1920s. Whenever my parents undertook a renovation project, I was fascinated by the drawings and blueprints. My grandparents' place in New Hampshire, though, was a 1765 farmhouse—and because of its history and quirks, so much more exciting than our home. Like the typical American farmhouse, it had undergone much reframing and reshaping over the centuries. It was wonderful to me, though, that the essential layout, original fireplaces, floorboards, low ceilings, and small windows had somehow survived. The core shared all the historical information of a museum room. But the house was still full of life—and still evolving.

Given my interest in and sensitivity to the experience of architecture from childhood, it seems funny now that

PAGE 2: A new, bracketed entry with a projecting roof reinforces the loose symmetry of this nineteenth-century house, carrying it squarely into the twenty-first century. PAGE 4: The moldings and varieties of fluting applied to the massive wall planes of this New York triplex bring its lofty entry into human scale. PAGE 8: For a quick sketch of my personal office workspace, I picked up the colored pencils and pen at hand. PAGE 10: New brackets, newel drops, windows, and doors help open and frame the view to the harbor beyond.

I had never thought of becoming an architect until, my sophomore year at Yale, I walked into an introduction to architecture class, just intending to check it out as one class among many. A slide of Louis Kahn's floor plan for the Yale Center for British Art happened to be up on the screen as I settled in. The professor, Alexander Purves, was saying, "We're going to study buildings. We'll ask questions like, 'Why is that column placed where it is?' 'Why are these rooms shaped the way they are?'" I intuitively knew the answers. But this notion of thinking analytically about buildings completely captivated me.

Yale in the mid-1980s was a great place to be an architecture major. The emphasis then was on the ideas and motivations behind a design, irrespective of style. Thomas Beeby was the dean. César Pelli, the previous dean, still lectured. Postmodernists on the faculty were searching for ways to bring back a consideration of traditional architecture, beauty, form, and ornament and felt a responsibility to study these topics with a rigor that had been absent for a while in academia. Kent Bloomer's class on ornamentation emphasized its intellectual grounding. Vincent Scully's lectures on the history of American architecture were a revelation. So were Robert A. M. Stern's on pride of place. No matter what the design, the focus was always on studying the site, the setting, the owners, the social aspects, and the converging of all the factors that made these houses possible.

Though my interest was centered firmly on the classical and traditional, the focus on form, shape, program, and ornament gave me many tools to look at traditional and modern architecture, to learn as much as I could about the lessons and solutions both approaches offered, and then put into practice. Once the Pandora's box of this intellectual approach had opened, it began to dawn on me that not only was the subject, the pursuit, so much larger than I had realized, but there were endless ways to study it—to absorb the lessons of the built tradition, to savor its precedents, to filter that evolving knowledge through my own changing experience—more than enough for a lifetime.

After college, a school friend and I traveled to England and then New Delhi hunting down buildings by Edwin Lutyens, then around the world through Southeast Asia and the Pacific Rim. Back in New York, I found myself unexpectedly at Parish-Hadley, which became a five-year education in how people want to live, and using the tools of architecture and design to facilitate that: how to shape a house and a room to work for a party, just the family, or a single person; how each room functions; how to lay out furniture; how to deal with an elevator; how to zone an apartment—what is private, what is public, what is perfect for the purpose—and so much more. These ways of living, I gradually realized, were fundamentals an architect should know when designing a house. I was learning how axes, view corridors, and sight lines create the order to enable better living. The Parish-Hadley experience was like studying the tools and tricks of the trade with a master painter, such as as how to use burnt sienna and Prussian blue because the combination makes the shadows pop.

Before heading to graduate school at the University of Texas at Austin, I spent a year in Brian McCarthy's office learning more about creating homes that exceed expectations and dreams. And once back in New York after graduation, following a brief stint at Davis Brody, I landed in Bob Stern's office, which I call my finishing school because it is where, over the next six years, I learned to be an architect. I briefly soaked up more experience at B Five Studio and another two years at Ferguson & Shamamian before becoming a principal at Hart Howerton. Six years later, in 2010, it was time to launch my own firm, which I did in partnership with Bob Miller, who sadly died in 2014.

This education still holds. In unlocking the mystery of how architecture does what it does, I continue to embrace the wonder of it all. No house I design is a copy of another house, yet each relates to the others in the way it speaks to the essence of place. My approach tends to be scenographic and, in its way, theatrical. Whenever I illustrate an idea, the plan is key, but I emphasize perspective because it captures and communicates the awe and beauty of the dream more immediately, especially to those clients not schooled in the language of plans. I use sketches and watercolors to distill the elemental idea, the essential feeling of place, the explanation of where I am and what I am seeing.

A few projects in these pages are renovations of late nineteenth- or early twentieth-century houses and apartments, and their reference points of inspiration are organic. Others built from the ground up take cues from the tropes, eccentricities, and pleasures of the American Shingle style translated for today. Still others trace their foundational ideas to more contemporary models in the architectural continuum. Always, each house contains multitudes in terms of past precedents and modern inspirations. Always, each house is intended to suit the client's particular lifestyle and the way we live today. I work from the broader to the more minute, sketching out the house's larger gestures all the way down to the procession of the entry, the plan, and the way the plan connects everything within the house to the surroundings and also creates a progression so that the joy of the reveal becomes an ongoing daily experience.

The way I think about and develop any project at any scale—but especially a house—follows from my education and my experience. All of the images, ideas, and influences, from the earliest through the most modern, are descendants of the classical tradition. Everything comes from something else, and so I always want to know more, to learn more, to discover more. What remains in the mind or the mind's eye as well as what gets lost along the way shape my understanding and insights for my clients. There are endless different ways of framing the world. Architecture is so many things, but it is also always for me a journey to discover where the idea of home begins.

# PLACE

Place is everything, encapsulating inspiration, conception, and completion. Comprehending and creating the idea of a "here," the physicality of a site, a built response to it, and the relationship between the two, can traverse many paths.

My personal sense of place, though, tends to dwell in the emotional and metaphysical. When a particular "where" resonates with wonder, a certain gravitas pervades our experience. For me, traditional architecture at its best excels at organically responding to an environment and endowing a structure, its spaces, and its surroundings with the indefinable qualities that make being there memorable and moving. The effect usually has little to do with style or ornament, but everything to do with the grammar, syntax, and vocabulary of the architectural language, and what its nuances can achieve in the way of expressing the rootedness that characterizes the indelible connection to an individual, the immediate surroundings, and the wider world.

My favorite places may seem simple at first glance. I love the hillside groves and the single cypress tree beside stone stele that the ancient Italians—Tuscan, Etruscan, Roman—set up to commemorate a victory, a loss, or a happening of religious or mythical import. These destinations, so essential in their architecture, reveal the human capacity to shape something meaningful in the landscape, to make a lasting mark. Furthermore, the paths we follow to reach these sites are not just part of the larger construct, but places unto themselves. The experience of this totality becomes fixed in the mind's eye and palpable and enduring in memory. The power of media to communicate much about these places obviously feeds into our understanding of them. Nothing, however, surpasses the reality of being there.

César Pelli used to say, "When you do a building in a city, you have to be able to figure out that place in fifteen minutes." Perhaps this is true. Maybe it is possible. It is certainly compelling to think that the spirit of a place is comprehensible that quickly. This is why holding on to the sense of wonder remains so important. To capture the spirit of place in a building in such a way that the structure will fit into its context and have its own identity, though, requires analytic and critical skills honed to penetrating accuracy, and the skills to use that understanding to shape the built work.

Much of what I do as an architect involves building metaphors. The paradigm of possibilities continues to broaden and deepen as I study and learn. This is why it is so meaningful for me to delve into the classical world. Understanding the siting of the Parthenon or the temples at Delphi, for example, may not directly influence the design of an apartment interior or the contours and floor plans of a house. But that knowledge carries with it an awareness of spatial potentialities that bear on our modern sense of place, and how we want to experience it and live in it. This creates a rich connection to the "here" and the "who," an architecture that enhances the engagement to the place.

Staying open to the emotional response to a site, walking it, looking carefully, experiencing its contours and countenance with all the senses—these are the first questions that architecture asks and then carries through in its making.

PAGE 14: The effervescence of watercolors captures an idea and essence of place—in this case, an imagined coastline. RIGHT, CLOCKWISE FROM UPPER LEFT: Metropolitan Life Insurance Company Tower, New York, by Napoleon LeBrun & Sons; on the beach in Rhode Island; Río Malleo, Argentina; Torre dell'Orologio, Venice; a view of the Weekapaug Inn, Rhode Island.

# HOUSES

SHELTER IS ONE OF THE FUNDAMENTAL PURPOSES OF A HOUSE THAT EMBODIES A CONNECTION BETWEEN INSIDE AND OUTSIDE. BUT HOUSES ALWAYS OFFER ANSWERS TO HOW AN INDIVIDUAL CLIENT WANTS TO LIVE. THE QUESTIONS COME FIRST. THEY ARE ENDLESS, AND INTRINSIC TO ARRIVING AT THE BEST SOLUTION FOR THIS PLACE. DESIGN EVOLVES FROM THE INSIDE OUT. TO ORIENT A HOUSE TO PEOPLE AND PLACE, I EMPHASIZE STRONG AXES, WINDOW PATTERNS, PROPORTIONS AND PLACEMENT, and overall harmony created by organically interrelated geometries. Axes and sight lines are my organizing principles, the ties that bind the interior to the exterior in a way that feels intimate and safe. Windows provide another type of correlative. They are the most immediate connection between two conjoined landscapes for living, within and without. Because the fenestration frames the views, its placement is critical, as is the way the pattern and proportion of the glazing resonate with a house's nested geometries.

Old houses still have so much to teach about elegant solutions to the quotidian activities and challenges of daily life, not least about maximizing the flow of light. Before gas or electricity, architects developed countless clever responses to assuage the atavistic human homing instinct to seek the light: houses a single room in width, glass transoms, glass doors, skylights, laylights, and so on. All these spatial devices remain relevant today for modern reinterpretation, as do other signature inventions of more recent prior eras.

I had a profound experience visiting a friend who owned one of Frank Lloyd Wright's Usonian houses. Perched just below the top of a hill, the house looked through a forest to a valley. In the bedrooms, continuous horizontal windows framed a slot of the woods. Neither ground nor sky was visible. The horizontal section of trees transformed the wall into something like a Japanese screen. Lacking a ground line and horizon, it read as an object. And as light and shadow shifted across its surface, and the leaves fluttered in the breeze, the windows became a living screen.

There are unique moments throughout every house I design that form part of its character: a square window inside a cabinet that offers a glimpse of the valley or field beyond—small, yes, but more than an Instagram moment; a diminutive private dressing room window with an almost pinpoint-focused view of the trees in a house otherwise tied to the landscape with enormous glass expanses; an aperture that frames a mountain in the transition space of a mudroom, like a loving tap on the shoulder to say, "Hey, I am right here."

Architecture provides an infinite spectrum of ways to be in the world. But I am always in search of the best answer. This means listening to the client, and to the place, and to the landscape. A sun-loving client might inspire a wide-open interior and double-height windows open to the surrounding environment. Another client may love light but prefer the less-direct exposure of covered outdoor spaces and deep, shaded porches. Whatever the desire, however seemingly simple and innocuous, it inevitably affects the design profoundly.

**PREVIOUS SPREAD:** A peaked roofline within a wooded valley strikes a primal chord of home.

Bishop Berkeley House 1728
Newport, RI

# TO PARAPHRASE POET WALT WHITMAN, EVERY HOUSE CONTAINS MULTITUDES.

Architecture today cannot help but channel its past lives, especially when, like this Southampton, New York, property, the idiom of the exterior emerges from roots firmly planted in the classics.

This property—main house, pool house, and garage/party barn—was designed to live in contextual comfort with its "house neighbors," which date roughly to the 1880s and provided the catalyst to our thinking. Strict setbacks and the desire for a house that unfolds on three sides to living and entertaining spaces and a large backyard dictated the placement and orientation of each structure on the one-acre lot. In overall geometry, modeling, massing, and details, the buildings—particularly the three-floor, ten-thousand-square-foot residence—take cues from the Queen Anne Shingle-

style–era houses that surround it, as well as the cottages that exemplify the late-nineteenth-century Shingle-style inventions by H. H. Richardson, Peabody and Stearns, and Clarence Sumner Luce. Aspects of this residence's floor plan, specifically the long interior axes with shifts from room to room, slip in echoes of Frank Lloyd Wright's early-twentieth-century Prairie-style houses. With the client's sophisticated appreciation of multiple styles of architecture and love for a see-through house, I celebrated the modern ideal of the infinite vista with massive windows, glass bays, and wide room openings that nod to the Farnsworth House, Mies van der Rohe's iconic mid-twentieth-century glass box.

Knowing that the blanket of shingles would calm any quirkiness, we co-opted not only the fanciful nature of the late Queen Anne–style neighbors into the modeling and form making of these structures, but also the decorative objects, ornament, and details that form the overall appearance of their facades. The massively overscale windows with divided lights offer another comment on the

PAGES 22–23: Sketches of this house alongside precedents by H. H. Richardson, Peabody and Stearns, and Robert Venturi hint at inspiration's alchemy. PAGE 24: Defining forms emerged early. PAGE 25: Plantings by Michael Derrig of Landscape Details enhance the stair tower. PRECEDING SPREAD: The parti is traditional, with an entry tower and balcony flanking a central dormer. PAGE 28: A preliminary sketch posits the breakfast room as a classical folly. PAGE 29: Flanking lanterns above echo its window configuration.

1880s, because by then, glass manufacturers were producing much larger expanses, which in turn allowed the architects of the period to heighten the connection between the interiors and the outdoors. Here, the traditional meets today through these windows where light and the framed visual connections to the landscape knit together the entire property.

The organization of this house clearly differentiates front from back. The ground floor plan is a straightforward, cross-axial cruciform with entry, living room, the husband's office/study, dining room, kitchen, breakfast room, family room up front, and powder room and mudroom in the back. Stairs with Chippendale-inspired fretwork, another updated 1880s reference through Italian mid-century, ascend to a grand, central second-floor hall with guest rooms to the right, and children's rooms, primary bedroom, and the clients' dressing rooms to the left. The enormous T-shaped window signifies the central axis that runs like an artery through the house, while carefully modulated connections to the large windows balance openness and privacy. The lower level houses a game room, wine cellar, and two more guest rooms as well as mechanical storage.

The interior architecture tends to the minimal, with restrained white oak millwork, rift and quartered white oak floors, incised plaster walls, and flat moldings with some profiles at the crown. On the main floor, we articulated the tray ceilings with beams, paneling, and strapwork to differentiate the individual volumes. In the private spaces of the second floor, height restrictions mandated that we shape the ceilings up into the roof structure to acquire more loft.

This property gathers history's continuum into its architecture. Dressed in traditional clothing, it is designed for modern living at the core.

**LEFT:** The floor plan's strong axial orientation creates directional clarity and an easy sense of flow throughout, including from the kitchen to the breakfast room to the pool beyond. The interior decoration is by Stewart Manger Interior Design. **FOLLOWING SPREAD:** The architectural ornament on the rear of the house with its shingle patterns, brackets, and Chippendale-inspired railing takes cues from this house's Queen Anne Shingle-style neighbors. The garage/party barn at the far end continues the conversation.

ABOVE: The sweeping roofline of the garage/party barn nods to another project that gave rise to the idea for its distinctive shape, which resembles the hull of a boat and hints at the lofty, swooping ceiling within. OPPOSITE: The balcony off the primary bedroom overlooks the pool house and a private gated garden abutting the study below. The architecture of place here emerges from the specific combination of shingled massing and white painted details.

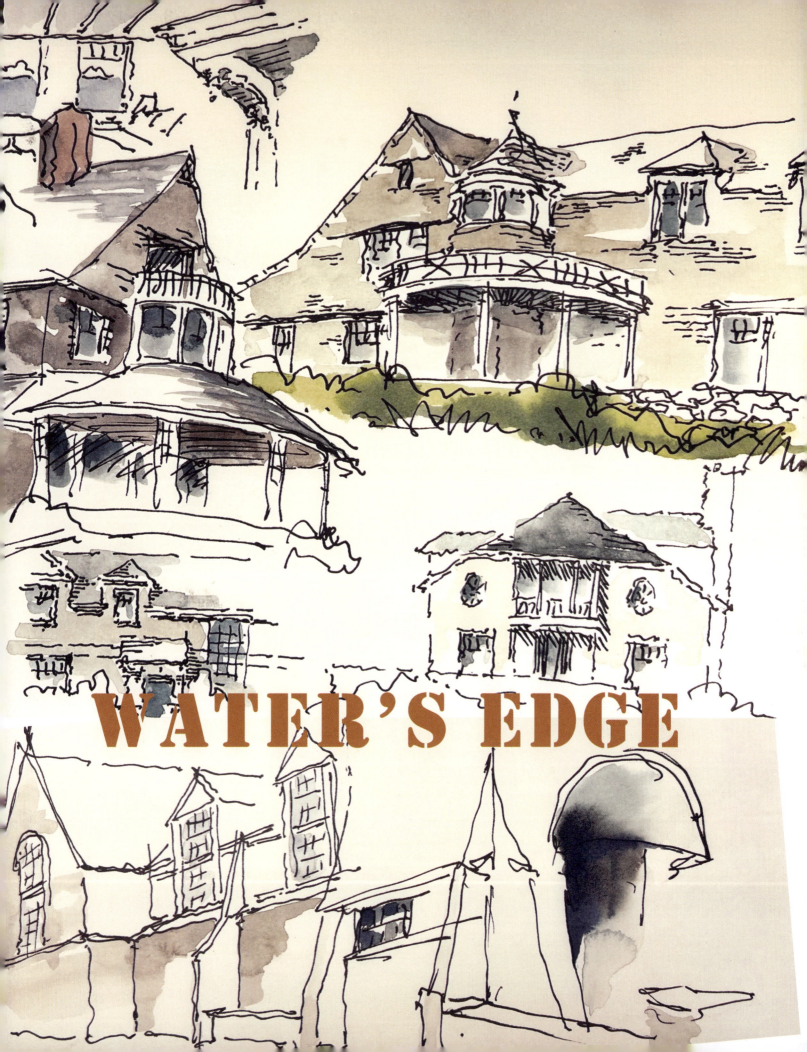
# WATER'S EDGE

THE LANGUAGE OF ARCHITECTURE COMPELS INVENTION. WHILE THE GRAMMAR OF STRUCTURE ADHERES TO STRICT RULES FOR OBVIOUS PRACTICAL REASONS, THE VOCABULARY THAT SPEAKS TO STYLE CAN BE INFINITELY INDIVIDUAL.

American Shingle-style houses like this beloved longtime family homestead on the Massachusetts coast tell the story of such complexities and contradictions. This house lives at the more formal end of the Shingle-style spectrum. A conglomeration of an 1880s core and later additions—including ours—the exterior exemplifies a quietly exuberant, traditional New England Dutch gable with a taut composition of tower, porch, and windows. The clients wanted this renovation to celebrate its character, and the family history reflected in its forms and materials while enhancing it, inside and out, for generations to come.

The ground floor's interventions, though not insignificant, consciously feel timeless to carry the memories forward: The profiles of new windows, casings, and doors, for example, match their existing counterparts. Replacement materials like flooring mimic but improve on the originals. More importantly, the existing relationships among the large rooms remain, with only subtle tweaks to bring in more light, improve the flow, and connect to the landscape. The entry hall, on axis with the porch, steps down to the living room, three sides of which look to the harbor; here the clients specifically requested we replace the shiplap wall panels, which were in perilous shape. A few imperceptibly deft changes carved out the intimate library. I also repurposed the former kitchen into the dining room, which now connects directly to the exterior through new double doors in the stone tower; converted the adjacent onetime family room into the kitchen and breakfast room, in the process opening views to the harbor; enhanced the existing storage capacity at the back of the house; and inserted an elevator.

The expanded space created by our large porch addition plus the reinsertion of a quadrant of the house removed in an earlier renovation allowed us considerable flexibility, especially on the second floor. Here, the extra square footage facilitated the introduction of a back hall with grandchildren's rooms, bedrooms, and a nursery, as well as the reallocation of existing space for the primary bedroom suite with the clients' individual baths and

PAGES 36–37: Sketches of this house and several random neighbors became the renovation's harbingers. PAGE 38: A little serendipity: The rear entry gate echoes the tree canopy overhead. PAGE 39: A painting of the porch conveys several of the site's defining features—wall, ancient tree, and shore. PRECEDING SPREAD: The revised main entryway proceeds from a new entry court through an architectural framing of the harbor vista, enhanced by the work of Martha Baker Landscape Design. PAGE 42: A Dutch door replaces the former portico. Cullman & Kravis transformed the interiors while keeping history present.

# THE CALCULUS OF RENOVATION MAY INVOLVE REIMAGINING EXISTING ROOMS FOR OTHER FUNCTIONS AND DETERMINING THE ARCHITECTURAL MOVES TO MAKE THE CHANGES MANIFEST.

dressing rooms. It further permitted the reconfiguration of the tower bath as well as a shared bath flanked by two guest bedrooms above the new covered porch.

The second floor was particularly dim thanks to a windowless, double-loaded corridor that ran down its center. To bring light into the darkness, I introduced a back stair with a capacious skylight that runs the length of the roof. I also added windows that flood the back vestibule and the hall with sunlight.

Embracing a house's vestigial life can lead to the quirkiest yet most convincing architectural solutions that, though of the moment, read as if they had always been there. The rounded door openings to the semicircular upstairs bath are a case in point. The happily eccentric, but sense-making space that is the primary bedroom is another; here, the removal of a flat ceiling lofted the room up into the peaked roof structure, creating arches on either side that do not quite line up, as well as a funky small door that slips in under the eaves. These kinds of choices enhance character, especially with the Shingle style. Ultimately, knowledge of the idiomatic language of architecture guides intuition and invention.

PAGES 44–45: New windows, doors, ceiling beams, and shiplap in the living room reimagine and enhance the original. PRECEDING SPREAD: Built-in bookcases and a new mantel help transform this former dining room into a family room. Interventions like new built-in glass-fronted cabinetry aided in converting the original kitchen into the present dining room. OPPOSITE: The kitchen and breakfast area are entirely new, but the cabinetry nods to the past iteration.

RIGHT: This bath, shared by second-floor guest rooms on either side, is the happy outcome of an opportunity in search of a solution. Originally, this space was an exterior sleeping porch. The expansive wraparound porch addition below created the opportunity for its enclosure and conversion to its current purpose. The windows suggest a ship's cabin; mahogany details and the floor's wide painted planks reinforce the sensibility. FOLLOWING SPREAD: The 180-degree wraparound porch addition at the tower beckons the family at all hours for dining and conversation, which has transformed the way they live in this house. PAGES 54–55: Over a century or more, this house gradually expanded along the waterfront; the oldest portion is on the right. The separate small structure, called the Think House, was refreshed as part of this renovation.

Villa Stein, Garches, France, Le Corbusier 1926. Car, road, house, landscape. Modern geometry and transport in a suburban landscape. An abrupt, flat fronted façade like a Peruzzi palace in the countryside Giorgiano with loggia commanding center, visitors, a shop decking

House in the flood plain in Bangkok Thailand stilts floating above the water. Structure and materials expressed clearly.

Farnsworth House flooded in May 2020. Iconic home in land that regularly floods. Placed high, as part of Mies' design to float above the water. Now everyone concerned about it. Ironic

Neutra House California, San Francisco. A favorite Carolyn Jay for its aesthetic, playfulness, refinement, and its own lean existence

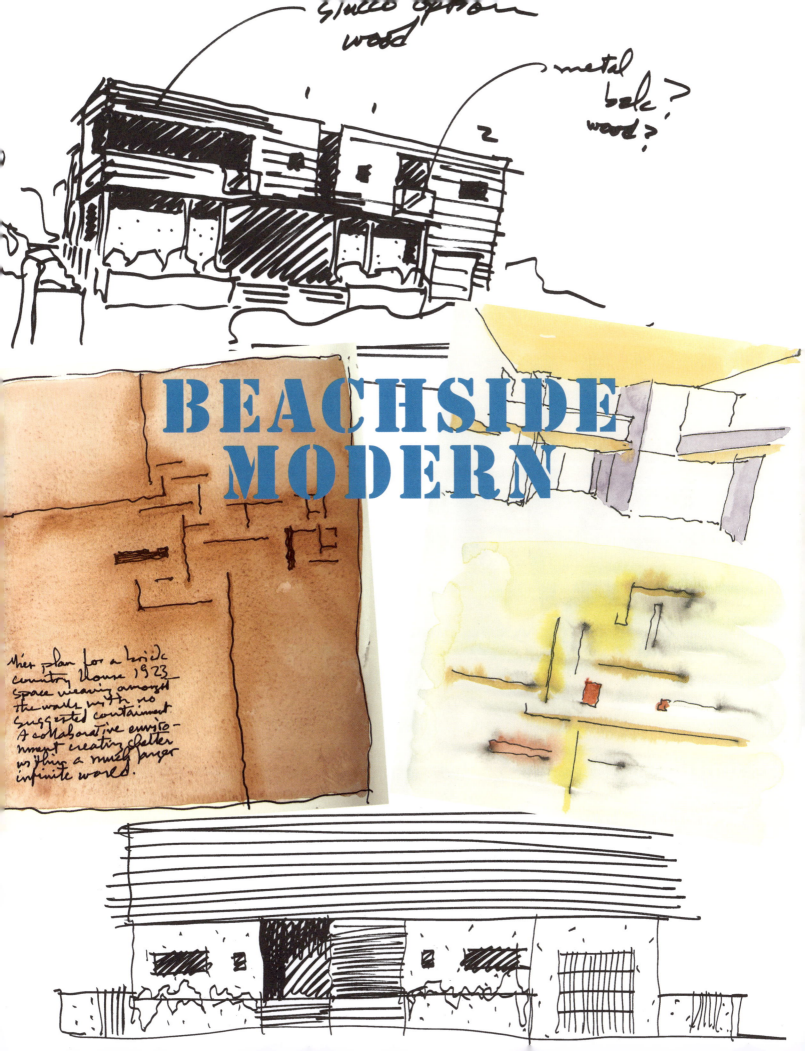

# BEACHSIDE MODERN

THE IDYLL OF PLACE FOR SO MANY OF US SPRINGS FROM GOLDEN CHILDHOOD SUMMERS ON REPEAT IN THE SAME SPOT. THAT IS CERTAINLY TRUE FOR THIS YOUNG FAMILY,

PAGES 56–57: Le Corbusier's Villa Stein; a typical house on stilts in Bangkok, Thailand; a Neutra house; and Mies van der Rohe's Farnsworth and Brick Country houses filtered into my approach to this modern beach house. PAGE 58: Technical sketches of this house's cedar screening system clarified the possibilities. PAGE 59: The front door offers a view to the backyard; a sliding cedar door pulls out to close off the entry from curious passersby. PRECEDING SPREAD: The choice and placement of fenestration, plaster, and cedar screening on the front facade maximizes the flow of light into the interior and privacy from the street. Landscaping is by Gibney Design Landscape Architecture. RIGHT: Cedar planked ceilings, trim, and baseboards carry the exterior materials into the interior. Both structure and visual statement, the Venetian-plaster-finished wall resembling corten steel—devised in collaboration with Bella Mancini, the client's interior designer—runs from the basement to the second floor.

who have flocked for years to the same old community on Long Island's South Shore as their parents and grandparents, a hamlet where the everyday rhythms of sun, sand, and surf feel bred into the bone. When the time arrived to build their own family retreat, they landed just half a block away from the beach. They wanted a house inspired by the Miami aesthetic of the wife's youth but softer. The stucco, glass, and cedar house we built evolved out of my initial response: "What if we do a modern house, but wrap it in cedar as a nod to the Northeast?"

Twentieth-century precedents that pioneered the open plan—Mies van der Rohe's mid-century Farnsworth House among them, but especially Le Corbusier's very early Villa Schwob and Dom-Ino House, and later Villa Stein and Villa Savoye—inspired my initial sketches. As these clients repeatedly advocated for a center front entrance, it became clear that they were imagining a traditional delineated floor plan of discrete, light-filled rooms behind doors for privacy, all clothed in modern garb.

The front door opens to an entry hall and central stair that leads up to the bedrooms and down to the playroom. Straight ahead is a double-height great room, the airy nucleus of the house that holds together the dining room, library/sitting room/television room, study, kitchen, breakfast porch, outdoor porch, and back terrace and pool that array off it. Also on the ground level are a guest suite with its own entry, a back stair to the basement, a powder room and closet, and a mudroom off the garage. Upstairs, the primary suite encompasses a sitting room and balcony that overlooks the great room, as well as the kids' rooms, all set into cedar niches.

I tend to take what I think of as a painterly approach to architecture projects, creating gestures that make the most of each moment. The main staircase here is a case in point. A slotted space between two towering walls finished in a Cor-Ten steel–like Venetian plaster, it frames the sky

**OPPOSITE**: Surmounted by a ribbonlike swath of skylights, the stairwell becomes a lightwell channeling daylight through the interior from the top of the house all the way to the lower level. **FOLLOWING SPREAD**: The compression of the entry foyer vaults into the double-height living room, where perpendicular balconies play off one another. The interior balcony focuses on life inside the house; the exterior balcony overlooks the activity in the backyard. Both aid the flow of natural light throughout.

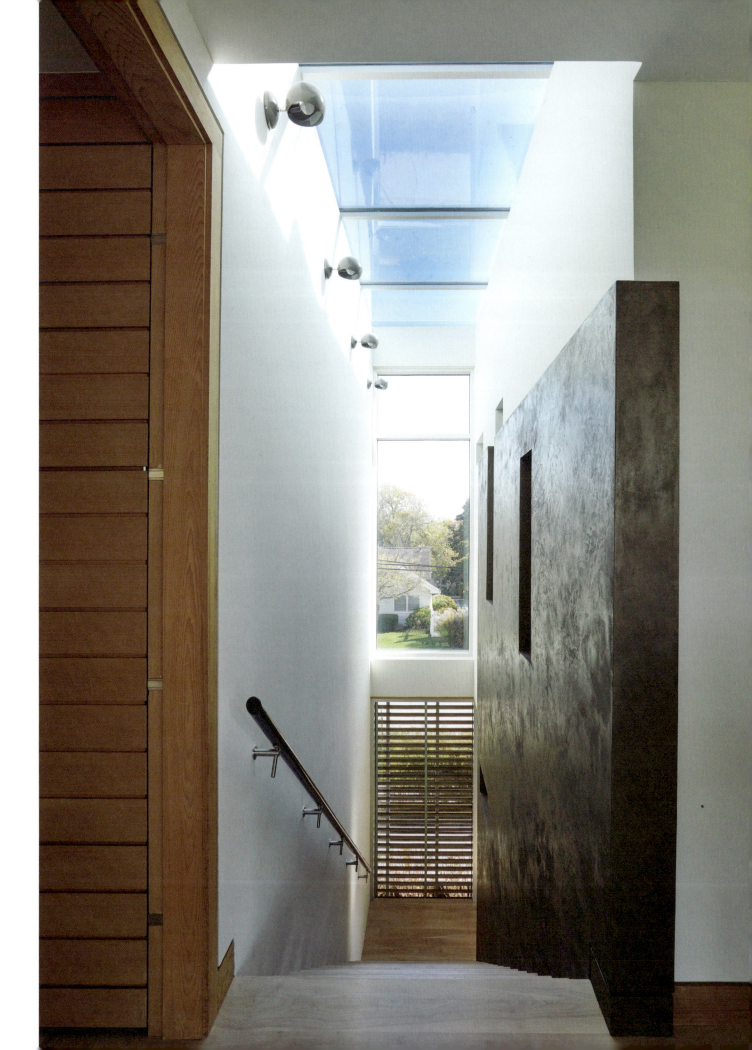

## MATERIALS ARE INTEGRAL TO A HOUSE'S ARCHITECTURAL EXPRESSION BUT ALSO CONVEY THEIR OWN MEANING. WHAT SAYS SUMMERHOUSE MORE CLEARLY THAN CEDAR?

and looks to nature while directing shafts of light. The balcony/mezzanine defines yet another slot, an open transept that connects the front of the house to the back, all the way through.

The exterior evolved from the floor plan and the need for privacy, which dictated the rationale for the placement of stucco, cedar, and glass on both the front and rear facades. We always intended to veil the entire street-facing expanse, particularly on the first floor, from prying eyes. The front door, an abundance of glass, incorporates a retractable cedar screen that pulls across to obscure the interior from view. The primary bedroom's clerestory windows provide both transparency and discretion. The cedar slats let in the light, while serving as a privacy screen. The floor-to-ceiling window that terminates the second-floor hall suggests transparency, but screening at railing height precludes visibility from the street. The back facade is another story altogether: completely open, and without cedar, it takes on the spirit of an open-frame structure.

As mash-ups go, the "Miami-modern-aesthetic-meets-the-Northeast" may initially seem unexpected. But for this family, and this community, it is a perfect fit.

**PRECEDING SPREAD:** The cedar planks shape the dining area and differentiate it from the other functions of the great room. The sliding door on the left leads into the family room.
**OPPOSITE:** In purely material terms, the exterior of this house is stucco with an attached screening system of cedar louvers for privacy. This balcony projects off the primary bath, allowing bathers a view out to the landscape while occluding visual access from the exterior.

As modern as the exterior of this house appears, its interior follows a more classically inspired organizational logic; in other words, it celebrates discrete rooms rather than a strictly open floor plan, notwithstanding the great room on the first floor. The upstairs hall doubles as a gathering and lounging area for the kids, and in that way adheres to the classic Victorian idea of a second-floor living room. Each of the kids' bedrooms opens through a cedar plank niche, which in series creates a visual and spatial rhythm along the hall's length.

ABOVE: This corner of the kids' living room overlooks the backyard. OPPOSITE: The primary bath is a study in using materials, shapes, and pattern to energize a space without overwhelming it. Frosted glass windows and a skylight ensure luminosity with privacy. FOLLOWING SPREAD: The front and back of the house are related yet distinct. Cedar slats shade the back porch, while window walls connect the rest of the living spaces to the landscape. A glass pool railing offers function without visual obstruction.

# ONE DELIGHT OF AMERICAN ARCHITECTURE LIES IN ITS CAPACITY FOR REINVENTION. THE AMERICAN SHINGLE STYLE ARGUABLY EXEMPLIFIES THE APEX OF THIS HAPPY MUTABILITY, AS THIS NEW JERSEY PROPERTY DEMONSTRATES.

PAGES 78–79: Sketches of the house posit ideas for the front and back facades, pool, and massing details. PAGES 80–81: The front entrance of this fierce Shingle-style house stands proud to the street; its expansive shaped roofline with gables and various dormers reinterprets many predecessors in the vernacular. James Doyle Design Associates was the landscape architect. PAGE 82: The process of drawing the interiors helps focus perspective on architectural decisions. PAGE 83: The slats of the stair balustrade, in combination with the windows and skylight above, choreograph an animating play of light and shadow over the course of the day. Fawn Galli was the interior designer. RIGHT: Instead of a dedicated dining room, the clients opted for a front entry hall expansive enough to do double duty as necessary. Sliding glass panels create the necessary separation from the front door on those occasions.

PRECEDING SPREAD: The language of this house is strictly rectilinear; there is not a single curve anywhere in the architecture. Simple stepped paneling activates the wall surfaces and reflects the fenestration details. ABOVE: In the breakfast area off the kitchen, the doors fold away for a seamless transition to the patio beyond. OPPOSITE: From the rough sawed board of the cabinets to the enameled steel hood, the kitchen's combination of materials recalls the arts and crafts period.

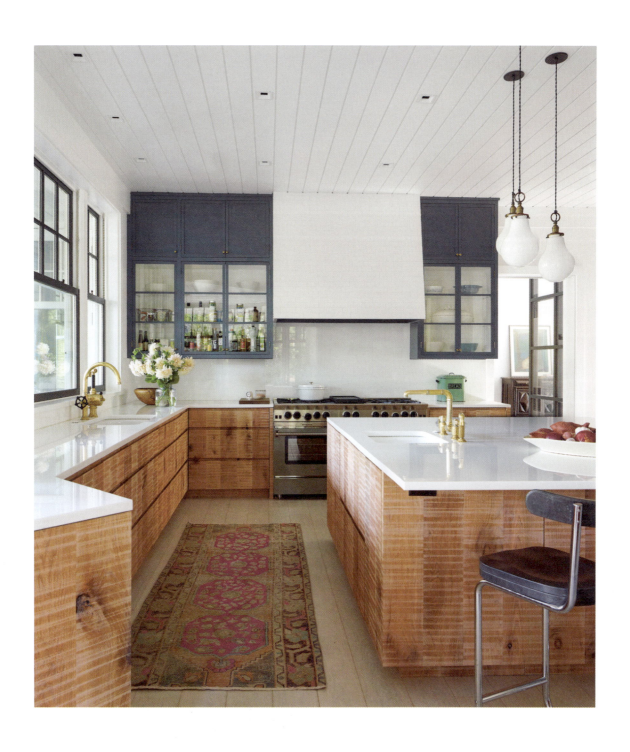

**RIGHT:** For this family of avid readers, a reading room was a key component of the program from the genesis of the project. As the project developed, this room evolved into its octagonal shape just off the party space and around the towerlike steel-clad fireplace. The steel tongue that extends from the hearth across the floor like a rug was inspired by Finn Juhl. The deep banquette is expansive enough for every member of the family to lie down and read, or nap, or just hang out together. **FOLLOWING SPREAD:** The rear facade, informed by a long tradition of triple-gabled English arts and crafts style designs, centers axially on the pool. The salt/pepper-shaker tower on the left houses the reading room at ground level and the primary bath above. The round chimney on the right, which anchors that portion of the structure, provides balance, though asymmetrically; the gentleman's study occupies the third floor.

These clients love the style's picturesqueness, enough so that they specifically requested it for the residence and pool house they planned to build on their two-and-a-half-acre lot in a historically significant suburb. They also registered an interesting caveat. Feeling that the style could skew cute, they wanted a "tough guy" version. "What about black shingles?" I asked.

Every architect draws on a treasury of influences learned over time, many neither chronologically contiguous nor from the same traditions. Precedents serve as a conceptual springboard for me, not an exact corollary. Consider Norwegian houses clad in wood siding charred with a technique similar to Japanese shou sugi ban, for example. These suggest one possibility for a house sheathed in black cedar shake. But here we ultimately used stain. Edwin Lutyens's turn-of-the-twentieth-century three-gable houses such as Tigbourne Court and Homewood provide food for thought for another, the kind of gracious suburban home with center entrances and central axis symmetry these clients envisioned. Louis Kahn's 1955 Trenton Bath House, which has intrigued me since my college days, came immediately to mind as a catalyst for this property's pool house.

In a house of any style, but arguably even more so in the Shingle style, the floor plan gives rise to the exterior forms. It certainly did here.

These clients wanted to keep their living spaces deliberately straightforward. They vetoed a dedicated dining room, so we created an entry hall large and detailed enough to double for the purpose. The clients, who entertain often, needed organic circulation pathways among the living room, lounge, bar, and reading room, well-placed fireplaces to serve as focal points, consciously framed views, and seamless access to the landscape. We carved out a kids' area on the ground floor with a homework room and lower-level play spaces connected by a spiral stair; adjacent to this is the lady of the house's office, which overlooks the porch through a round portal window. The kitchen, breakfast room, pantry, and powder room hold their own on the other side of the main stair, which lands upstairs at a skylighted book nook. The primary suite with a balcony opens off the second-floor center hall, as do the kids' bedrooms, the kids' sitting room, a laundry, and a gym

**OPPOSITE:** At the top of the stairs, a reading nook with a built-in book niche nests neatly under a gable; the skylight and dormer windows wash this space with ample natural light during the daytime.
**FOLLOWING SPREAD:** The massing and details of this house are a study in balance and asymmetry, as the pair of flanking chimneys makes clear. The architectural details inform the landscape design as well; here a line of pleached trees mimics the central gable's pediment brackets above.

# A BUILDING MAY BE IMMOVABLE, BUT TO EXPERIENCE ARCHITECTURE REQUIRES MOVEMENT. APPROACH, REVEAL, AND ARRIVAL ARE ESSENTIAL TO THE DEFINITION OF PLACE.

space/guest room. The gentleman's office is lofted into an aerie in the sky on the third floor.

Much of the inspiration for the exterior's dialed-back, modern take on traditional American Shingle style worked its way into the interior finishing and detailing. Strong gestural moves like horizontal board siding with a V-groove ceiling, subtly stepped wall paneling, flat moldings, raw wood beam work, and the kitchen's rough-sawed cabinetry set the tone.

When clients share their dreams, wants, and preferences, it makes such a difference. The house that comes into being expresses them and how they want to live, and architecture in a way becomes the least of it. These clients became involved in all aspects of the design, including the little touchpoints. None of us really knows where inspiration comes from. But listening to the clients and then merging my ideas with their desires? It is a joy to build on this type of foundation.

**PRECEDING SPREAD:** With a structure inspired by Louis Kahn's Trenton bathhouse and a spirit informed by Slim Aarons's photographs, the pool house incorporates a kitchen, dining, and lounge areas. The floor extends directly onto the pool deck. **RIGHT:** The pool house, which sits at the far terminus of the central axis organizing the entire property, serves as a focal point for the layered rear landscape and view from the main house.

# BY THE BAY

PRECEDING SPREAD: The rocky Atlantic coast is one of New England's singular features and in its way, a true definition of place. RIGHT: The renovation of the exterior of this Shingle-style grand dame included shifting numerous windows to align properly with the interiors designed by Bunny Williams, as well as expanding the window over the new front porch and door with side windows, front entrance portico, and entry court. PAGE 106: The new entry now greets guests with a view straight through the house to the harbor beyond. PAGE 107: In drawing details, much information and direction emerge.

**ARCHITECTURE IS ALWAYS A COLLABORATIVE EFFORT SPARKED BY A SOCRATIC-STYLE DIALOGUE OF QUESTIONS AND ANSWERS WITH THE CLIENTS ABOUT THEIR NEEDS AND DESIRES.**

If the project is a renovation of a long-owned and dear house, like this historic American Shingle-style home on the Massachusetts coast, any sensitivities about the extent and style of metamorphosis obviously factor in. These clients, for example, had loved and lived in this house for many years, and had clear ideas about how they wished and needed to reimagine it for their twenty-first-century lifestyle. Specifically, they wanted to recast the exterior into a vision of the exuberant 1880s original—think round towers, a double gable on the front center entrance, Chinese Chippendale tea pavilion, porch dentil moldings, curved shingles going into window openings, and more—and open the interiors to the water vistas.

Unsympathetic additions in the 1920s and 1950s with wide picture windows had extended the footprint of the house parallel to the waterfront. At some point in this concatenation, the main entry shifted to the side of the house, the twin peaks of the roof moved off-center, and the sleeping porch was lost. My goal for our reimagining and restoration was to re-create the house as it might have been without any evolution over time. This meant centering an entry and porch on the twin gables, continuing a long porch open to the harbor, recasting the fenestration with windows shaped and scaled to relate to interior spaces renewed, reorganized, and reproportioned by a fundamental reconfiguration.

The new entry porch put the harbor immediately in view, created a direct connection to the living room, and a starting/landing point for what is now the ground floor's two-pronged circulation. One route extends from the living room and side porch, while the other do-si-dos through the library/TV room, kitchen, and mudroom.

The clients chose not to have a dedicated dining room, so instead a dining area nests by the living room fireplace. Part of the mantel and the room's exposed structural column existed. The rest of the living room we remade from the floor to the coffered ceiling with plaster shaped to look as if it came from the 1800s and slim moldings that snap in the corners, which are very much in the spirit of these historic Atlantic seacoast houses. This level of detail continues throughout.

**PRECEDING SPREAD:** In the entry hall, new wainscoting and crown molding ring the space and bring it into sharp focus. The crown molding is intentionally and appropriately minimal, like that found in late-nineteenth-century seacoast houses; in effect, it reads like a joint line at the meeting point of wall and ceiling. **OPPOSITE:** Windows now overlook the restored grand porch that parallels the harbor and wraps the house; the screened porch at the far end is one of the new additions.

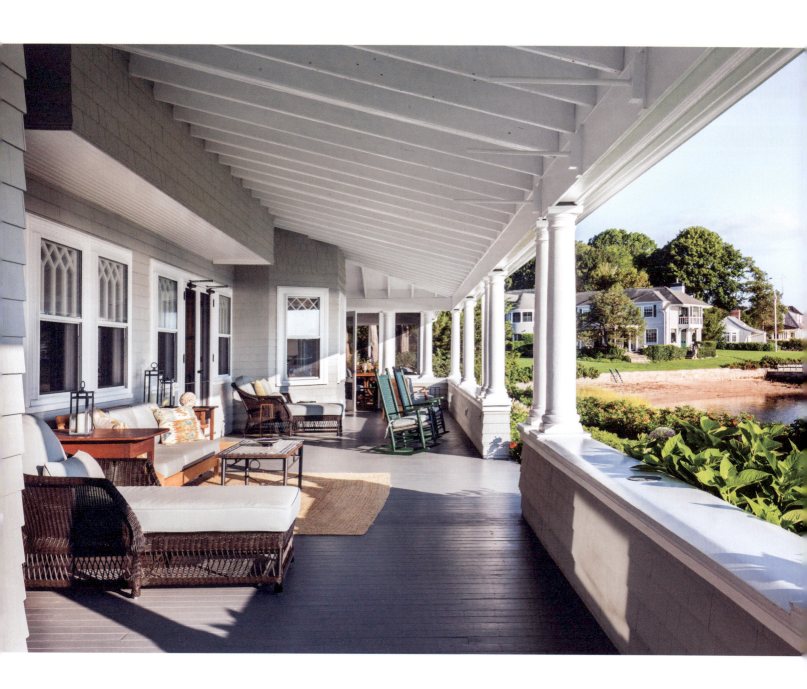

New architectural details such as crowns, baseboards, casings, and beams join those already present in the extant living room. All the additions and alterations took their cues from the existing structural column.

# IN RENOVATING A MUCH-LOVED HOUSE, IT IS IMPERATIVE TO BRING THE ARCHITECTURE INTO THE PRESENT WHILE KEEPING ITS ORIGINAL CHARACTER INTACT.

The clients spend considerable time in the kitchen, and often read at their kitchen table, so shaping this room as much like a library as a workspace made sense. Carving out an adjacent breakfast area and adding a screened porch gave the entire area a gracious unfolding. The truly transformative move, though, was repositioning the stand-up appliances in the pantry, so the kitchen now contains only a cooktop and sink, upper cabinets, and the bookshelves that give it its distinctive character.

The second floor is a pentimento all its own. The 1920s addition created a center hall with a bedroom at the top of the stairs. The 1950s addition, however, resulted in a rabbit warren of hallways, three smallish bedrooms sharing a bath, two other bedrooms sharing another bath, and a primary suite. Our rearrangement of this puzzle box resolved it into a quiet simplicity. The top of the stair now lands in a large windowed sitting area. We combined the three bedrooms into one, retained the existing louvered doors, replaced the 1950s glazing with charming half-round windows, and installed uniform fenestration under the eaves that adds flair with a 1920s feel.

When the challenge is to retain the character of a place, the instinct is always to hold onto as much of the past as possible. This is not always necessary—at least, it certainly was not here. Facets of this house carry its history forward, while new elements enhance its spirit.

OPPOSITE: These clients have spent a great deal of time over the years reading at the kitchen table, so it made perfect sense to find an architectural response for combining the dual function into a hybrid library/kitchen space. Bookshelves join delicate storage cabinetry for dishes on the upper perimeter to frame an axial view through to the fireplace. Other than the stove, sink, and dishwasher, which are built in here, the rest of the kitchen appliances and equipment now live in the neighboring pantry space.

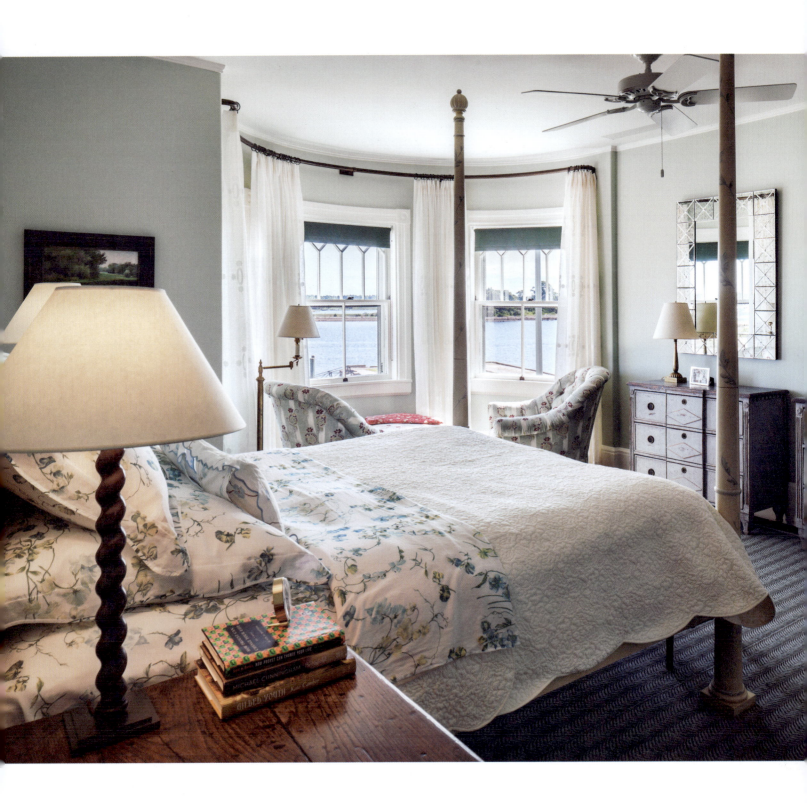

ABOVE: Sometimes just a new cornice and plaster walls are enough to refresh a beautiful space. OPPOSITE: The goal of our work on the primary bath was to create an improved, twenty-first-century version of the memory of its original classical look. The basket-weave tile floor, vintage tub and sinks, and ceramic tile walls resonate with its history, while the large glass shower and wide mirrored cabinets bring modern breadth.

ABOVE: The wraparound side entrance to the porch now lives where the front door used to be. The small arched window up above the new portico is also an addition.
OPPOSITE: A cottage on the property now functions as a garage; the brackets above its foundation provided inspiration for other projects. FOLLOWING SPREAD: With its open waterfront vistas and architectural eccentricities, this updated Shingle-style house becomes one version of the archetypical summer home.

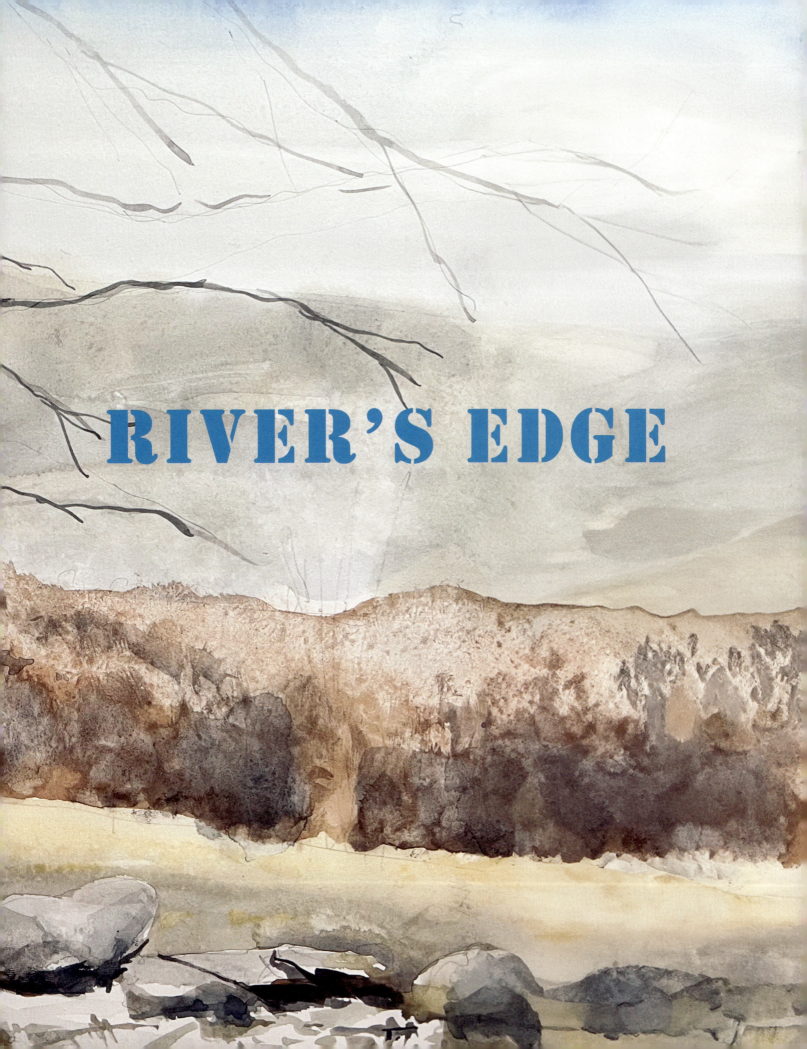

PRECEDING SPREAD: For centuries, Cornwall, Connecticut, has been an agricultural community; remnants of the old stone boundary walls thread this history through the landscape.
RIGHT: The drama of old architecture meeting new construction stands out with graphic clarity in these two adjoined structures, one a nineteenth-century farmhouse, the other, a reinvention of the barn vernacular with enormous plate glass windows, screened porch, and metal roof.

**ARCHITECTURE'S CAPACITY TO CREATE A BRIDGE TO THE NEW WHILE RESPECTING THE PAST IS ONE OF ITS MANY FASCINATIONS. THAT IS WHY BRINGING A HOUSE LIKE THIS PERIODICALLY REBUILT CONNECTICUT FARMHOUSE FULLY INTO THE TWENTY-FIRST CENTURY PRESENTED**

such an intriguing challenge. Its original Federal portion dates to the early 1800s. This core was more or less intact, but had suffered multiple additions over the centuries, the most recent being in the 1950s. These clients, who had rented the house for a decade before purchasing it, loved its quirks and eccentricities. But they wanted a proper working kitchen, a capacious party space, better views and improved conditioning (the house still had its single-glazed windows), a more organized flow of rooms, and so on.

The family was also very clear that whatever metamorphosis we crafted, it had to stay true to the spirit of the original place. Before we began, they handed me a copy of Thomas Hubka's *Big House, Middle House, Back House, Barn: The Connected Farm Buildings of New England*, which chronicles how farmhouses like this one evolved to meet each new generation's needs. The norms and traditions of this Connecticut region,

**OPPOSITE:** Except for the shell of the original Federal house, all the architecture is new. The variety of materials helps break down the scale of additions that essentially doubles the size of the original house. Double-height doors close off the barn when desired. **FOLLOWING SPREAD:** Removing the wall of the stair hall facilitated the creation of this living room overlooking the valley. **PAGES 130–31:** A new tin ceiling helps reflect sunlight through the cozy, low-ceilinged kitchen. Fawn Galli was the interior designer. Michael Trapp was the landscape designer.

# WINDOWS ARE CONDUITS FOR DAYLIGHT. BUT THEY ALSO SPEAK TO TIME, PLACE, AND ARCHITECTURAL PERSONALITY THROUGH THEIR FORM, SCALE, AND PROPORTION.

for example, dictated that the farmhouse face the road, stand a set distance from it, and, when backed up to a hillside, as here, expand sideways. We wanted to honor these conventions, as well as revive and incorporate the almost lost language of the property's stone walls as a thread of continuity.

The reshaping began in the entry stair hall and adjacent living room, where I opened the spaces and jiggered doors to shift the long views into focus and tighten the connection to the exterior. This reconfiguration relocated the kitchen, created powder rooms, a bar, and a series of small but necessary interstitial spaces, including a mudroom. Accreted with the addition were a screened porch, a second side entrance, a back entrance for several of the upstairs bedrooms, and a Pullman-car-like library expansive enough for ten or twelve people to hang out, with fold-away doors for a seamless indoor/outdoor connection.

The second floor was a crazy quilt of bedrooms off an interior hall with a single window. To tame this higgledy-piggledy situation, I reshaped it into a rational, T-shaped circulation axis with a grand, arterial bedroom hall that

OPPOSITE: All the new double-hung windows in the house echo the six-over-six configuration of the original fenestration even when their proportions differ. Here, the windows band together to create a panoramic view of the hillside into which this kitchen/family room is immersed. The new wood stove that helps warm this space also provides a remembrance of things past, as it were, as a memento of what could have been in a previous life of the farmhouse.

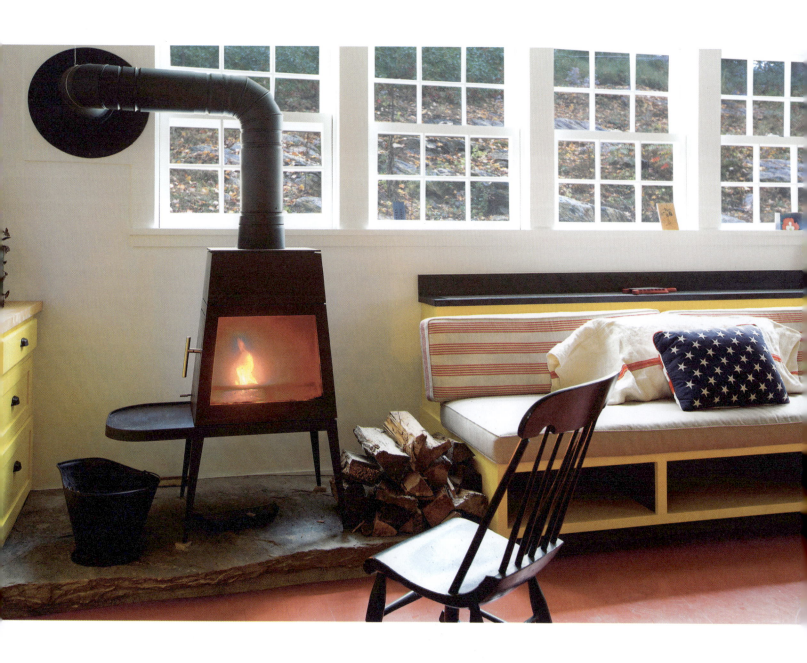

This is one of the few houses where the clients insisted that I choose all the colors, including the shades of eggplant and butter that bring so much warmth to this resultant space from the renovation. The intention here was to evoke a farmhouse interpretation of a Pullman car. The firebox is original, but all else, though rustic and old in appearance, is new.

OPPOSITE AND ABOVE: The demolition process uncovered layers of old paint on the upstairs hallway's floorboards, a serendipitous discovery, and a record of past layouts. Built-in bookcases and a seating area by the window make this a welcoming upper hall. FOLLOWING SPREAD: The commanding loft space of the primary bedroom overlooks the fields below. The ceiling beams conceal all the mechanical systems, and a skylight directs the sun's beams onto the bed.

# EVERY PROJECT POSES A PLETHORA OF QUESTIONS THAT THE ARCHITECT STRIVES TO ANSWER. OCCASIONALLY, THE BEST SOLUTION IS TO LEAVE THINGS AS THEY ARE.

meets a back guest room hall, which also connects to the primary suite over the new party barn. In the process of reshaping these spaces, we unearthed layer after layer of the house's lived past in the surviving traces of painted floors, which generation after generation colored to their preference.

The new kitchen anchors the barn addition, where an American vernacular form meets today's window wall, with massive black doors. Time's echoes reverberate, too, in the fireplace, which replicates a Rumford model the clients had seen in an early-eighteenth-century house and found charming. Though we toyed with painting the exterior red, we opted for black stain to remind the family of their days in France, where some salt barns have for centuries been painted black on the east facade to warm with the sunrise and white on the west facade to stay cool in the afternoon.

In country houses like this one, the structure mediates between man, nature, and time. At each point, the plan provides an organizing principle, manifesting the idea of place through gestures both large and detailed. Modern and traditional marry in sensitivity to the moment.

The topography of this site, and specifically its exposed bedrock, presented something of a challenge: To blast? Or not to blast? This was one of those times when the better decision overall was just to let things be. The exposed bedrock creates a mesmerizing insight into the nature of place from the dining room area in the great room of the new barn.

ABOVE: The modern aesthetic begins to assert itself in the new primary bath, which centers on a large plate glass window to take advantage of the view. OPPOSITE: The screened porch added to the farmhouse stretches the full length of the older structure. FOLLOWING SPREAD: The entire house is nested into the hillside, and from this vantage point lives up to the nickname for the garage, "the hermit's cottage." At the right, an understated entry leads into the garage below.

# SUBURBAN PAVILION

# IN ARCHITECTURE, SMALL PACKAGES CAN PORTEND WONDROUS THINGS—LIKE THIS POOL HOUSE PAVILION IN WESTCHESTER COUNTY,

New York. These clients love and celebrate their historic property, which Grosvenor Atterbury designed in the 1920s/1930s. They cherish Atterbury's glorious Spanish Revival-style main house, as well as the tennis court and pool. And they delight in the role the property plays as a nexus for family gatherings with friends. But the existing pool house proved inadequate to their needs from day one. When they opted to build a new structure rather than renovate, they wanted to do so in a way that would speak graciously to the property's legacy and to today's inventions.

In addition to the pure fun of delving into Atterbury's language, razing the

PAGES 146–47: Sketching Grosvenor Atterbury's main house aided in formulating the architectural language for the pool pavilion inspired by the Spanish Revival buildings of Atterbury's contemporary, Addison Mizner, and other Palm Beach precedents. PAGE 148: The pavilion echoes the main house's palette. PAGE 149: Black-and-white sketches helped determine the necessary architectural moves to achieve the desired shadows. ABOVE: The left-hand structure houses a living room, bedroom, storage, and laundry. OPPOSITE: White oak fluting simulates drapes around the arches. LC Studios was the interior designer.

old pool house gave us a chance to site the new structure to create coherent, logical relationships with the property's other constructed elements, gardens, and extraordinary views. The L-shaped pool house we crafted—a Spanish Revival–influenced envelope with grand arched openings on three sides and an art deco modern glass box grafted onto one end—embodies a unique combination of the past and the present. The traditionally inspired portion houses the large living room, with one end of the L encompassing an extra guest bedroom and bath, changing area, and laundry, and the kitchen in the glass box at the other.

As planned, the structure is itself a bit of a transformer. When the overlapping, double-arch doors pocket into their walls, the core of the space becomes an open pavilion in the middle of the landscape. We looked to Atterbury's oeuvre and Palm Beach with its contemporaneous trove by Addison Mizner for precedents, as well as certain of Carrère and Hastings's Gilded Age treasures in a similar language. Then we filtered all that information through a contemporary lens to simplify and modernize the period detailing. Chamfers, angles, and cuts in the parapet make light dance across the facade over the course of the day. The chimney riffs on the faceted columns of the existing house.

The interior architecture likewise incorporates pared-down, Palm Beach–influenced details, like Italian plaster walls and beamed, white oak ceilings (rather than pecky cypress), oak lintels, wood and tile floors, and ribbed wood door surrounds, almost like stylized curtains. The kitchen, glassed in on three sides and with glass cabinets as well, is on full display to the pool.

One of the beauties of Spanish Revival architecture lives in its use of the formal repetition of contrasting geometries as an organizing principle, which in turn offers remarkable flexibility to create and embrace the associated spaces that emanate from the footprint that results. Here, these include a courtyard with a fountain, a grotto for watching tennis, another covered space by the pool, a rustic path emerging from one side, and at the front, Sienese steps that cascade into the landscape. This small package? It opens up to the best of several worlds.

This patio, which overlooks the tennis court, lives under a planted pergola off the main space of the pavilion. The decorative tiles on the fountain wall are in keeping with the scenario inspired by Mizner's Mediterranean fantasias. The tiled door casings and floor continue the motif of decorative form meeting superior function.

OPPOSITE: The glass-box-like galley kitchen, the short end of the L-shaped plan, accretes a modern flourish onto the pavilion's architecture. In the living space, stone banding creates a planar field for the tile infill, adding an interesting layer underfoot. The porcelain wall sculptures were commissioned from Anat Shiftan. ABOVE: The bedroom offers everything a guest could need, including ample built-in storage and a wonderful view of the landscape. The artwork is by Robert Mars.

Topped by a small temple, a flourish to Atterbury's original designs for the chimneys, the architecture of the pavilion offers a paean to the ideas of openness and connectedness to its surrounding environment. The arches of the pool and the pavilion resonate with one another. A glass fence surrounds the pool so as not to obstruct the view.

# FOREST TO FIELD

# WHEN THE PLACES OF THE PAST RESONATE IN A CLIENT'S PRESENT, THE CONDITIONS ARE RIPE TO CREATE AN ARCHITECTURE OF DREAMS.

That was the case for this house in the Catskills on a vast site encompassing mountains, fields, and forests across thousands of acres threaded with the remnant stone walls of farmers. The clients spoke poignantly of formative joys—of hiking varied terrains and childhood experiences within Frank Lloyd Wright's remarkable midcentury houses—that very much influenced what we envisioned here: a house on one level, connected to and celebrating the land and

the landscape, with deep, gently sloped eaves to deflect winter snow and harbor summer shade.

For any American architect, Wright inevitably strikes a chord (and for me, not least because of our shared last name). But Wright was also a focus of my undergraduate curriculum. Vincent Scully, Wright's friend and champion, illuminated the man and his work in detail, from the mythos of the Froebel blocks to the Prairie style with its ideas of infinity and the late Usonian houses with their parti of rigid geometries. Wright's houses always hew to an essentially Victorian plan, with the fireplace at the center, a great hall, and offset rooms. This is certainly true of the Robie House and the no-longer-extant Welbie L. Fuller House and the Usonian houses, which, with several Lutyens's houses, were sources of inspiration here.

Investigating Wright's language was exciting because his vocabulary works so well with the large expanses of glass that are a defining feature of this house bridging the forest and the fields, as well as its wonderfully intimate rooms. The exterior asserts itself quietly through its elemental geometry and materials, specifically local New York bluestone and rift and quartered white oak. The facade incorporates three window types to engage the views in highly choreographed ways. Matching details inside and out tie the architecture and interiors closely to the terrain, and to nature.

The entire structure—three contiguous components, the middle one skewed—pinwheels around a gigantic double fireplace with a massive chimney composed of rock from the site. The circulation and public spaces occupy the uphill side, while the private spaces face the field and valley views. This solution appealed strongly to the client because, like so much of Wright's late work, and particularly the Usonian houses, it emphasizes the framing of vistas as they unfold along the house's footprint.

Arrival begins below the house, continues through the vine-planted pergola over the carport and flagstone entry path parallel to the structure, and turns to the front door, which opens into the kind of contained entry de rigueur in

**PAGES 158–59:** An initial inspiration sketch conveys the essence of the great room that has come to be. **PAGE 160:** The combination of stone walls and natural wood have a Catskills flavor. The brise-soleil melds influences from Le Corbusier and Frank Lloyd Wright. **PAGE 161:** This sketch reveals the chimney as the plan's center and centrifugal force—and the house's sentry in the landscape. **PAGES 162–63:** A slight shift off axis transforms the exterior's personality and the interior's panoramic views. **PRECEDING SPREAD:** The resolute stone chimney is integral to the interior. **OPPOSITE:** The dining room is an attached pavilion jutting into the landscape. Sarah Magness was the interior designer.

# WHEN THE CONFIGURATION OF A HOUSE PERMITS, NATURAL LIGHT CAN BECOME PRACTICALLY PALPABLE, AND, IN THAT WAY, MATERIAL TO THE ARCHITECTURAL EXPERIENCE.

a Wright house. A "left" turn is my fascination with Le Corbusier's never-built Maison Errazuriz with its butterfly roof, internal ramp circulation, and exploration of spatial compression and visual release. The introduction to place here converses with both. The tight, low-ceilinged vestibule vaults into a soaring, glassed-in great room of living, dining, and kitchen areas overlooking the limitless landscape beyond. In addition, the house embraces a pantry, primary suite, and two guest rooms, as well as the clients' office, which is positioned to function like "command central" and doubles as a crafts room and a place for grandchildren to sleep over.

If a house can be a metaphor, this house expresses the architecture of a life, and the passions, places, and spaces experienced along the way as it continues to emerge in the landscape.

PRECEDING SPREAD: With expanses of glass on three walls, the views from the great room encompass both the forest and the field—both sunrise and sunset. OPPOSITE: With windows above the kitchen, the great room has natural light and views on all four sides. FOLLOWING SPREAD: Even as the house zigzags through the forest, the architecture aims to become one with the landscape in the way it hugs the earth and its use of characteristic local materials. James Doyle Design Associates was the landscape designer.

# INSPIRATION

Inspiration comes from anywhere and everywhere, but what I love about the discipline of architecture is that there is always more to see and learn. The tradition is its own wellspring in a way. Architecture for me is a pragmatic endeavor, a continuum of evolving ideas and expression.

    The primal aspects of structure—safety, warmth, revelation, celebration, remembrance— are the genesis of all the many languages of building, whether a perfect temple by Ictinus, an early colonial American fort, or everything before, between, and after. These are the same visceral needs that, regardless of style or location, the vocabulary of residential architecture addresses. As with any language, the greater the immersion, the better the understanding of its nuances, the more powerful the meaning it can convey.

    I love the thrill of encountering something in or about the designed world that is not just new to me, but that sparks the curiosity to delve deeper. I can vividly remember the moment in graduate school, for instance, when a brilliant professor opened my eyes to the nesting of geometries within the composition of an elevation. This way of seeing entirely transformed my perspective and intellectual framework. The realization that this generative device had been passed down through millennia, generation after generation, from the ancient world to Queen Anne architecture to Lutyens and even the present day? Exhilarating. My senior thesis project on Erik Gunnar Asplund's Gothenburg courthouse addition drove this reality home. I had always loved Asplund's neoclassical architecture, but the deeper I dove into the project, the more I began to realize how transitional a figure he was because he also loved modern architecture, and did a great deal with it, too. He grew up immersed in the tradition of his era, but by virtue of the time in which he lived, found himself thrust into the emergence of modernism. His work charts the pathway he found to marry the two, as his addition to the Gothenburg courthouse makes clear. The original structure dates to the sixteenth century, and the addition, to the 1930s. From the outside, the two display all the hallmarks of their age. From an interior perspective, the addition incorporates the latest technology of its era in lighting as well as laminated surfaces. Yet from the standpoint of the plan, the two are the same: a courtyard building adjacent to a courtyard building.

With its various and evolving ways of making and doing, of organizing information and tried-and-true systems, the tradition of architecture is where inspiration reliably lies. The blessing of our time is that architects can practice in a variety of styles, everything from Shingle style to Georgian, from Federalist to Modernist. My approach is to treat each as its own dialect, to learn what its specifics are capable of, and what they convey. As I understand each of these various ways of thinking and communicating in greater depth and detail, I grow ever more excited about each project I design.

The immersion into a place or a culture that is foreign to us forces us to absorb, to learn how to maneuver, to gain the facility to connect—not just survive. I love this process. It is the most telling way I know to find the best answer for each client, each place, in this time.

PAGE 174. Baldassare Longhena's seventeenth-century Santa Maria della Salute epitomizes the Italian baroque. RIGHT, CLOCKWISE FROM TOP LEFT: As Italian Renaissance masterpieces go, the Villa Caprarola by Vignola sets an exceptionally high bar, as does Winchester Cathedral for the English Gothic; James Gibbs's eighteenth-century Radcliffe Camera at Oxford for the English baroque; Trajan's Forum in Rome, a classical model from the 1st century AD; and the Byzantine Church of Santa Costanza, one of Rome's fourth-century wonders.

My time in the Parish-Hadley architecture department just after college was my first real exposure to addressing how spaces function, creating comfort, and what the tools of the architectural trade can achieve. Just three months into my tenure there, I was drawing house and apartment plans, furniture layouts, and essential details such as eighteenth-century inspired consoles, Greek key friezes, and cabriole legs, the sorts of human-scale details that inform the conversation between the intimate moment and the overall gesture that is essential to the design of beautiful, comfortable, functional living spaces. It struck me then that a set of essential architectural solutions—fundamental moves, as it were—exist for design and space planning, in particular.

People want to move around a home and its rooms in an organized fashion, without directions, so the procession and circulation within, as without, should be logical, easy, and organic. The front door, for example, opens into an entry hall, which should unfold into a living room, dining room, or gallery that connects these rooms and flows from them to the outdoor spaces and/or the views. I can still hear Albert Hadley chiding, "Don't put the door too close to a corner because it makes the space difficult to use and that corner all about circulation." When circumstances dictate such an awkward move, as will inevitably happen, experience and precedents offer options for dealing successfully with the difficulty. The force multiplier that comes from the combined skill sets of an architect and an interior designer exponentially increases the ability to get these fundamental spatial moves right, which in turn can lead to some uniquely felicitous results.

Every interior designer I have ever worked with looks for ways to use decoration to tie each space visually into the next, however subtly, so the home feels complete and coherent. On my end, this effort involves developing an architectural program that does the required knitting, giving the spaces form, devising the piece or pieces that will drive the rest of the design, and inserting the appropriate details. At the most basic level, these include sympathetically designed baseboards and cornices to demarcate thresholds, doors, and openings between distinct spaces and those in-between, and, of course, to shape the all-important connector that is a staircase. Should classical references make sense, the integrity of the details take precedent, so I will insert real nods to the period past with the geometries of the ornament.

The most special effect I can put into play, though, is to add in function so that every area will do more than serve its ostensible purpose. Sometimes this involves reallocating space not only to change fundamentally the way clients live in their interiors but also to improve the visual connections within and to the exterior so that the spaces feel larger.

Every interior starts in the architecture, as lines on a page, then as geometric definition and decoration. In the best collaborations, the boundary blurs between where the architecture ends and the decoration begins. Certain interior designers regularly introduce me to possibilities beyond anything I knew could exist, whether it is a material, or a type of lacquer- or stone- or metalwork. The wonder of seeing and handling these special, exquisite items, of finding ways to incorporate them into the architecture of the space we are creating together, makes the joy of design immediate. Pushing this limit of potential? It is a thrill and an honor.

# ONE OF THE BEAUTIES OF USING THE LANGUAGE OF CLASSICISM IS THE RANGE AND FLEXIBILITY OF MEANS IT AFFORDS FOR BRINGING HUMAN SCALE TO SPACES OF DIVERSE KINDS AND DIMENSIONS.

**PAGES 178–79**: The Lalanne objects in a Philadelphia apartment and others by Brian McCarthy captivate the eye. **OPPOSITE**: A riff on late Lutyens and American art deco suited the renovated entry foyer of the Philadelphia apartment by Brian McCarthy. **FOLLOWING SPREAD**: The solution to the issues of scale presented in this West Village triplex by Aman & Meeks, included the addition of fluting, pilasters, molding, and other classical architectural elements.

ABOVE: Ribbed glass set within a panel wall ensures both privacy and the passage of light from the entry into the adjacent living room of this Fawn Galli–designed Upper West Side interior. OPPOSITE: The forced perspective of this Foley & Cox–designed Park Avenue entry hall takes inspiration from Bernini's Scala Regia. The classical tradition often uses artwork within architecture—like the piece by Iván Navarro concealing the entry hall closet—to reinforce a sense of place and play with our sense of distance.

When reinventing a historic space like this turn-of-the-twentieth-century apartment by McKim, Mead & White for the present, sometimes the best solution is to enhance what already exists. In this collaboration with Cullman & Kravis, that was the approach taken for the grand entry hall, where raising the door and window openings—and C&K's addition of jewel tones and gold accents to the original ceiling—did much to modernize the space.

# IN REINVENTING THE ARCHITECTURE OF A RESIDENCE WITHIN AN EXISTING HISTORIC BUILDING, THE DETAILS OF THE FACADE CAN PROVIDE ENDLESS INSPIRATION.

**OPPOSITE:** One of the challenges of working on this West Village triplex with interior designers Aman & Meeks is that in its previous incarnation, it was simply wide-open gallery space. Every bit of the original detail, to say nothing of the rooms, had been deleted, so all the interior architecture from walls to moldings to ceiling coves and panel details is new. The created arches that mark the transitions from room to room take inspiration from the details of the exterior architecture and help tie the entire residence—inside and outside—into a coherent, harmonious composition.

This is the living room on the other side of the glass-paneled entry hall of the Upper West Side apartment on page 186 with interiors designed by Fawn Galli. The project was a complete gut renovation, with reenvisioned interior architecture intended to resemble prewar environments in its details and feeling. To that end, breaking down all the walls and reshaping several preexisting rooms into this main living salon refocused the newly created space onto the wall of windows with a panoramic view of Central Park, and offered the added benefit of bringing much more natural light deep into the interior. As for the architectural details, the client's previous residence in one of New York's classic prewar buildings provided both an appropriate language and a kit of parts for reference in creating all the new embellishments.

In this New York penthouse high above Central Park, a collaboration with the late interior designer Amy Lau, the image of an island in the Swedish archipelago of Stockholm provided a metaphor for the architecture. The shaped wood walls were inspired by country houses on the islands; the shaped plaster components took cues from Erik Gunnar Asplund's modernist projects from the 1930s. The windows slide open to access the terraces.

This apartment on Philadelphia's Rittenhouse Square with interior design by Brian McCarthy was another case of remaking and adjusting the existing historic architecture to meet the present moment with its desire for light-filled living spaces. Enlarging the openings on the window walls made it possible to gain shared daylight between the different rooms. New trim, floors, and details capture and reflect the light.

RIGHT: The renovation of this West Village triplex in collaboration with interior designers Aman & Meeks involved adding walls and rooms to transform the previous museum-like modern gallery spaces into a welcoming residence. The introduced arches between the rooms mirror the shape of the windows. The ceiling in this main living room is approximately thirteen feet high; with a high-gloss paint finish, it feels even loftier. FOLLOWING SPREAD: Prior to acquiring this Park Avenue residence, the client had a loft in SoHo. Our program here was to re-create the idea of that SoHo space in traditional garb with interior designers Foley & Cox. From an architectural standpoint, this meant reshaping the existing rooms off the entry into an open-plan loftlike space for an expansive living room and library.

**VESTIGES OF BUILT HISTORY PRESENT CLUES AND MYSTERIES RIPE FOR DECIPHERING AND TRANSLATION, WHICH IS WHY STUDYING THE PAST PROVES SO FRUITFUL IN DEVELOPING AN ARCHITECTURE FOR THE PRESENT.**

The wood paneling in the library of this McKim, Mead & White apartment on the Upper East Side with interiors by Cullman & Kravis is an entirely contemporary invention, created with a secret entrance to the primary suite and to conceal the mechanical systems. The panel details and the configuration of elements evolved from close study of the existing moldings, as well as the ideal of what the original might have been.

The library of this Central Park West apartment with interiors by Fawn Galli occupies one end of a large T-shaped room. The client loved the Philip Johnson–designed interiors of the now gone Four Seasons Restaurant in the Seagram Building. The mahogany veneered panels of that space inspired the wall treatment here.

**ABOVE:** There are infinite ways to design and detail paneling to suit a particular vision. For the library/music room of this Philadelphia apartment with interiors by Brian McCarthy, ebonized oak paneling detailed with brass moldings suited both the language of this space and the overall vision for the home.
**OPPOSITE:** In this Park Avenue apartment with interiors by Foley & Cox, focusing the architecture to shape axial views through the living spaces creates connections that instill comfort.

The bar of this Foley & Cox–designed Park Avenue apartment reveals the rich possibilities that come with combining French polished mahogany, brass moldings, and mirrored shelves.
**ABOVE:** Industrial gears inspired the U-shaped wood segments concealing a structural column revealed in the process of combining two smaller rooms to create this generously proportioned media room of the McKim, Mead & White apartment with interiors by Cullman & Kravis.

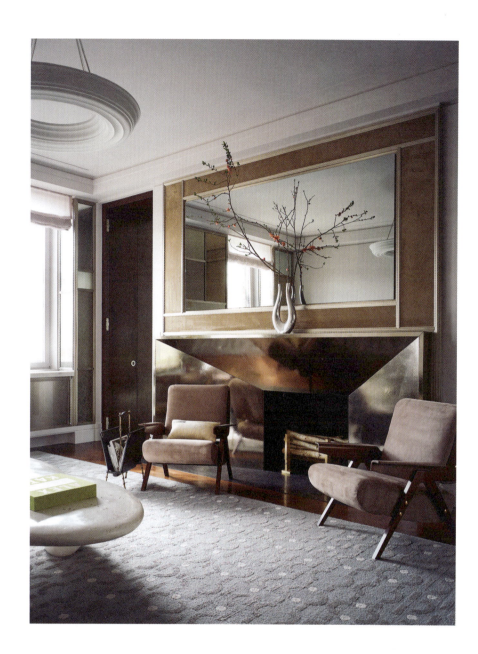

LEFT: Wood paneling with a warm patina transforms this newly created library and television room in the West Village triplex with interiors by Aman & Meeks into a quiet respite, providing a nice contrast with the rest of the bright spaces. Reflective wallpaper provides additional warmth in the evening. ABOVE: Craftsmen can make the difference. The sitting room in this Park Avenue apartment with interiors by Foley & Cox incorporates floor-to-ceiling mahogany doors, a television mirror framed by verre églomisé and polished nickel, and a mantel of polished, mirrored volcanic lava stone, all built by Rink of Paris. Though completely contemporary, this space resonates with echoes of art deco.

# IN SHAPING SIGHT LINES, FRAMING VIEWS, INDICATING PATHWAYS, AND DEVELOPING SPATIAL PROGRESSION, THE ARCHITECTURAL QUESTION IS ELEMENTAL: HOW AND WHAT TO REVEAL.

The Central Park West apartment with interior design by Fawn Galli is T-shaped, with the dining area occupying the bottom leg of the "T" set on axis with and visible from the entry. In addition to focusing the flow of natural daylight into the depths of the interior by expanding the vistas from room to room, the architecture had the additional goals of delineating distinctive spaces for separate functions within a comparatively open floor plan and molding organic pathways between.

This Fawn Galli–designed apartment on Central Park West previously had discrete rooms. The renovation removed the walls of the classic prewar space to open it up to light and the views of the park. The architectural detailing hews to the building's original period, gracing this contemporary plan shaped for a twenty-first-century lifestyle with a sense of history.

The dining room in this Philadelphia apartment with interiors by Brian McCarthy is a perfect square. Asymmetries abound within the clean, spare, very restrained architectural detailing framing the space and setting the stage for McCarthy's interior design to shine.

ABOVE: In this Upper East Side kitchen created in collaboration with Cullman & Kravis, the ceiling, reshaped in a continuous barrel vault, conceals mechanical systems stretching from the front to the back of the apartment.
OPPOSITE: This kitchen anchors one end of an Upper West Side loftlike penthouse with interior design by the late Amy Lau. The skylight centered over the island adds a vertical moment to the resolutely horizontal space. Deep, wood-lined window jambs, baseboards, and cabinetry details tie together the architectural composition.

Crown moldings, plaster ceiling details, wall panel configurations, and more: Every last element of the architectural detailing in this dining room decorated by Cullman & Kravis is entirely new and created to reproduce the effect of McKim, Mead & White's original, early twentieth-century space.

ABOVE: Natural daylight is always at a premium in Manhattan apartments, and its flow tends to drive much of the design decision-making. In this Central Park West apartment with interiors by Fawn Galli, the entry vestibule's ribbed glass panels allow for the breakfast area to share illumination from the living room windows. OPPOSITE: From the high-gloss-painted ceiling to the enameled metal cabinetry, subway tiles, and stained concrete floor, the kitchen surfaces bounce light through this internal space.

# THE PLAY OF LIGHT AND SHADOW ACROSS THE ELEMENTS OF ARCHITECTURE CREATES AN UNPREDICTABLE DRAMA FROM DAY TO DAY AND SEASON TO SEASON THAT ADDS AN INDEFINABLE POTENCY TO THE CHARACTER OF ANY SPACE.

Fluting of various dimensions brings texture, proportion, and scale to the stairwell and landings of this West Village triplex with interiors designed by Aman & Meeks. It also energizes each component of the overall spatial composition with the complex, always evolving interactions of illumination with form, shape, and line.

ABOVE: The shadow play across the architectural elements of this West Village triplex by Aman & Meeks contributed to their final determination. The entry hall's paneling details take inspiration from the stair halls of English country houses. OPPOSITE: The ironwork of the stair railing recalls the continuous fluting. PAGE 228: New glass doors, a tiled deck and stops, plants, and a walkable skylight transformed this lightwell into an oasis of an interior courtyard. PAGE 229: This enfilade ending in a mirror adds clarity to the floor plan and interior views.

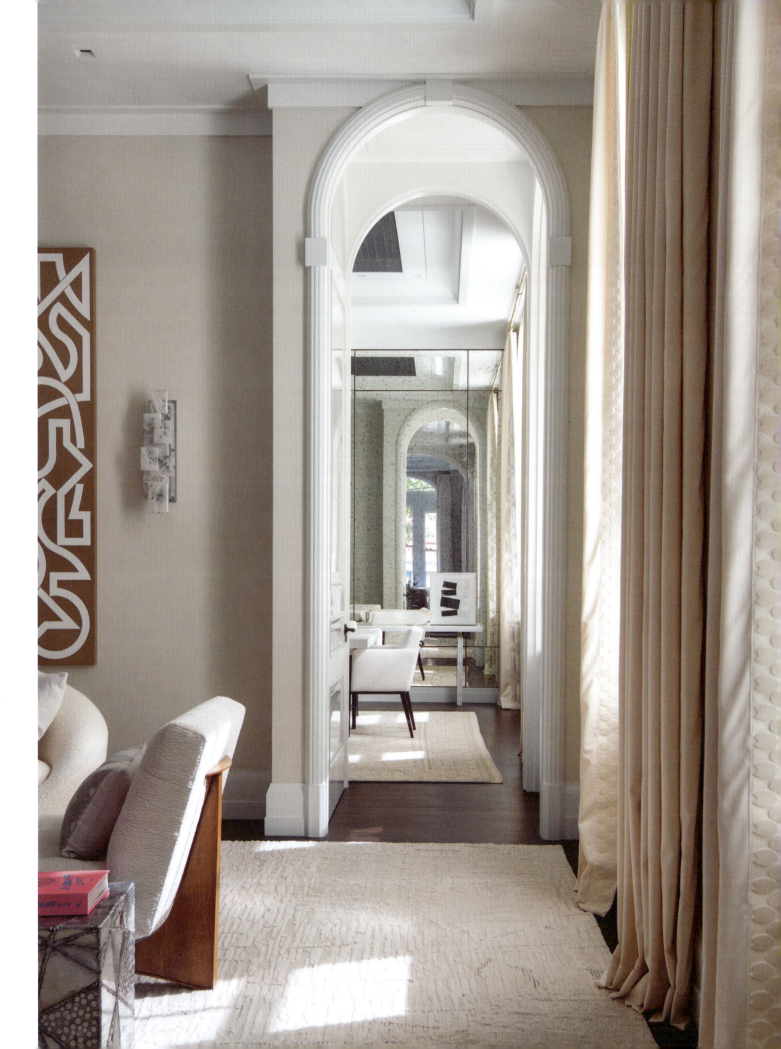

THERE ARE TIMES WHEN INTERIOR ARCHITECTURE SHOULD REMAIN IN THE BACKGROUND AND CONTRIBUTE QUIETLY AND UNOBTRUSIVELY TO THE OVERALL DESIGN, AND TIMES WHEN THE PREFERRED CHOICE IS TO USE THE INTERIOR ARCHITECTURE TO GO BEYOND FUNCTION AND MAKE A MAJOR AESTHETIC STATEMENT.

**PAGES 230 AND 231:** An architectural intervention in the form of a modern, steel-sheathed cube delineates and houses the transition space between the children's areas and the primary suite in the Park Avenue apartment with interiors by Foley & Cox. The cube encloses an entry vestibule to the primary suite and sits on axis with the main hall of the apartment, creating a clear view through the interior when the stainless steel doors are open. When the doors are closed, they soundproof the sequestered parts of the residence. **OPPOSITE:** The primary bedroom opens off the vestibule, a quiet retreat with the primary bath just adjacent.

**ABOVE AND OPPOSITE:** In the Upper West Side penthouse with spectacular views of Central Park and greenery all around, the animating architectural idea was the metaphor of the apartment as an island in the Swedish archipelago of Stockholm. The late Amy Lau designed the interiors. Planked walls, ceiling, and built-ins transform the classic 1970s greenhouse addition housing the primary bedroom into its own little island. Lau designed the bedside consoles and vanity in the primary bath.

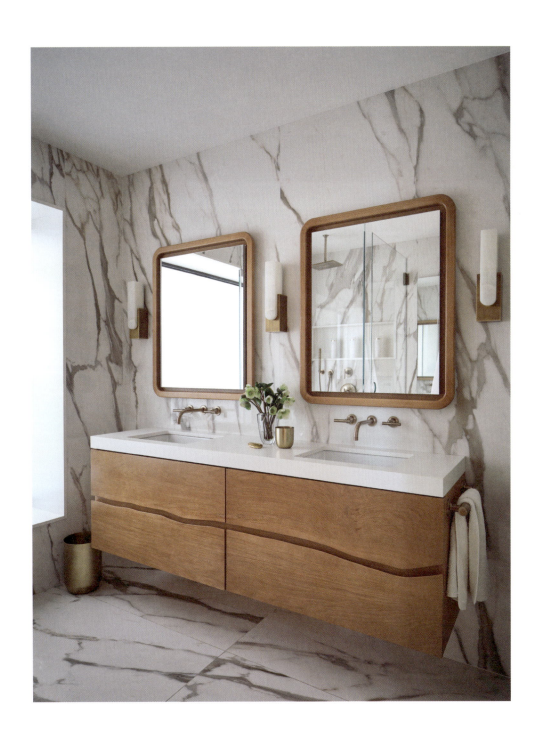

The primary bedroom in the Philadelphia apartment with interiors designed by Brian McCarthy offers a great example of design and architecture working in tandem. For the bed niche, the built-in bookcases, mirrored panels, center panel on the bed wall, dropped soffit, and casings all contribute to the elegance of this intimate space within a space.

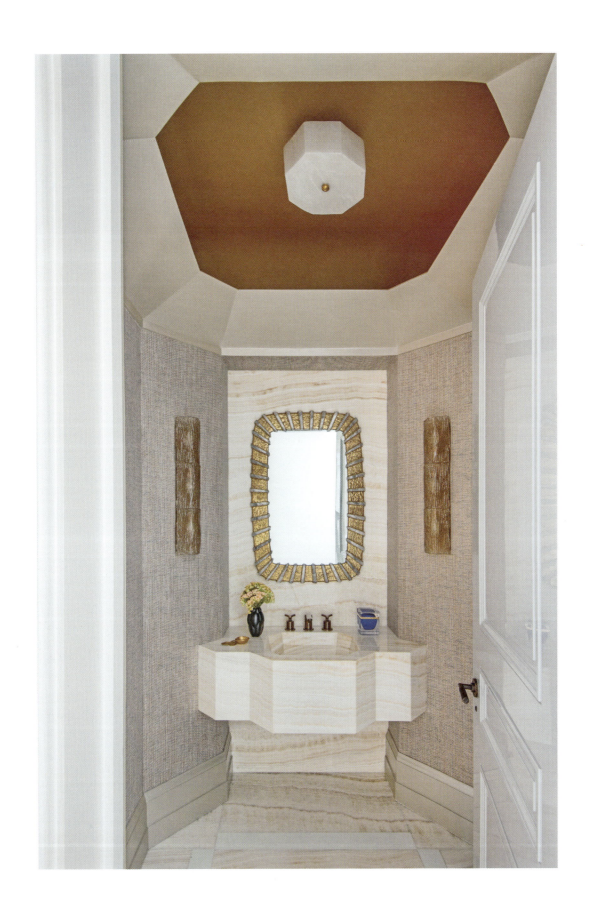

PAGE 238: Splendid materials can enhance even the most petite of powder rooms, as the two-toned highly figured marble slabs create a checkerboard in this Central Park West apartment with interiors by Fawn Galli. PAGE 239: The bold, octagonal motif expressed through the architecture of the recessed ceiling tray, onyx walls and floor pattern, and vanity transform this powder room in an apartment designed with Aman & Meeks into much more than simply a memorable statement about geometry. RIGHT: The polished nickel threshold, panel details, and door frames in the primary bath and dressing room in this Park Avenue residence with interior by Foley & Cox resonate with echoes of the suite's stainless steel entry. Sandblasted and ombré glass panels provide privacy at the entry, respectively, to the room and the shower. The closets feature panels of verre églomisé and wood.

ABOVE AND OPPOSITE: Simple shapes—basic geometries—sheathed in blocks of a memorably figured marble house the tub and shower, enhancing Fawn Galli's interior design for this Central Park West primary bath. Adding to the material mix are stained concrete floors, Venetian plaster walls, and a polished brass vanity.

# THE HAND

Something ineffable and mysterious happens when pen, pencil, or brush meet paper. The eye directing the hand sharpens the intellect, focuses the perception, and heightens the memory of the moment, the place, the experience. A quick gesture made on a napkin, casual or careful, or a seriously studied ink drawing, or a watercolor scene—for me these are the most direct and resonant means to decipher, record, and communicate essential architectural ideas. But more than that, they can capture something indefinable that enables me to remember the feeling in that moment. The line seems to link directly to memory.

A sketch can convey a thought so much more clearly and immediately than words can, so in the office, sketching is part of our practice. And we hone our drawing skills regularly. As in an art class, we might do a thirty-second sketch of an object, a one-minute study, and a three-minute drawing. Then we pin them up to see how each of us sees by analyzing the object of our focus, how we frame it, and how directly we reveal its essence.

My love of watercolor has only grown over the years. When I paint, I am trying to capture the feeling I have for a place, not a literal depiction, though the relationships of the colors, the shadows, and the intensity of the contrast might document the physical facts of place. I use watercolors to study an idea or to prepare for a project. My goal is to translate my sense of whatever has seized my interest onto paper to serve as the guiding genesis. When I am successful, the original idea survives intact through the relentless testing of the developmental process from raw sketch through repeated refinement to architectural drawing and building.

My travel sketches serve as inspiration as well as providing an internal frame of reference. In a recent watercolor of Santa Maria del Popolo in Venice, for instance, I tried to convey the effect of sunlight on the massing of the lush, warm travertine. At the time, I was thinking about whether there might be a way to make Shingle-style houses look and feel more Italian. This sketch prompted a "what-if" line of thought. Might it be possible to just focus on the effect of light and shadow on a facade of a house dressed in the warmth of shingles? The shadows might not make that house look Italian, but they absolutely offered another way to see shapes and forms.

How is it possible to translate an insubstantial feeling into a physical manifestation? How can a drawing capture the long history or evolving character of a place from its beginning centuries ago to its renaissance of contemporary expression? The communicative power created by the play of light and shadow never ceases to amaze. Dark trapezoids in a bright landscape? They are basic geometry. But as conceptions of shelter, they are also mutable to whatever traditions I want them to follow.

Holding onto the core idea of each project—what it is trying to achieve, what is important to it, how to celebrate it through the language of architecture in an elegant, powerful way—and holding onto these answers through the long process of its creation is essential. Understanding and showing the initial idea is what drawing, no matter the medium, does best, most eloquently, and with incredible economy.

PAGE 244: The landscapes of New Hampshire hold many memories for me. **RIGHT, CLOCKWISE FROM UPPER LEFT:** As does this view of Ravello, Italy; the massive form of Mount Katahdin, Maine; Quonochontaug Pond in Rhode Island; Lutyens's Thiepval Memorial to the Missing of the Somme in northern France; and the baths at Bath, England.

# THE FUTURE

A book is a retrospective act, a rare and enlightening opportunity to look back on completed houses and tell their stories. But the office always works on more projects than we are fortunate to publish. With ten to twelve on the boards at any time, a lively conversation is always underway about architectural ideas and their distinct expression.

Because of my love of classical architecture, and my desire to create architecture that lives in the now and the future, certain themes inevitably remain consistent from one project to the next, from one decade to the next. Some individual design solutions emerge because they meet the given moment and set of needs, while others, it is to be hoped, transcend time altogether. For me, these are the motifs and philosophies that carry the past into the present—the ideas and approaches I continue to examine now as I work, study, and travel, always expanding my frame of reference and point of view.

There is a special kind of fun involved in looking back to assess how these ideas have evolved over time as my professional skills, critical lens, knowledge base, and experience in solving the challenges of architectural design have continued to develop. Similarly, it is fascinating to see how, as time passes and the unique challenges posed by each project present themselves, my approach to making architecture—continues to undergo refinement.

Most exciting of all is to see how my thinking about architecture has evolved. Architecture is a profession of continual improvement. The learning is cumulative, and it never stops. Each project adds to the foundation of knowledge one can draw on for the tasks at hand and carry into whatever comes next. Certain skills, insights, and approaches only emerge with time. Age and experience bring with them a facility to solve problems in a way that would have been impossible a decade ago, much less as a young architect just beginning.

With the growth that occurs naturally during a career, the fundamentals become second nature. This is when it becomes possible to focus—really focus—on the aesthetic ideas without the inevitable compromises made while the skills, however strong, are still developing toward their peak. The best, obviously, is when the fundamentals and the aesthetics work in tandem and produce something new. That synthesis is the attempt in the three projects illustrated opposite, now in their formative stages.

OPPOSITE, TOP: A beach club on Long Island incorporates influences from the early history of Native American coastal shelters to the contemporary expression of American Shingle style. CENTER: The living room in a Georgetown, DC, town house updates the bas-relief friezes of neoclassical Gustavian paneled rooms with a nod to Kara Walker's silhouettes and John Trumbull's Revolutionary War–era paintings. BOTTOM: This house on Long Island is a modern mash-up of traditional Shingle style with the work of Paul Rudolph and Frank Lloyd Wright's Wingspan.

**SUMMER RETREAT**
page 22

**PROJECT TEAM:**
Christian Ricart, Ashley Walton, Gizem Bayhan, Eero Schulz, Adam Welker

**INTERIOR DESIGNER:**
Stewart Manger Interior Design

**LANDSCAPE DESIGNER:**
Landscape Details

**CONTRACTOR:** John Hummel Associates

**WATER'S EDGE**
page 36

**PROJECT TEAM:** Adam Welker, Julio Gavilanes

**INTERIOR DESIGNER:**
Cullman & Kravis

**LANDSCAPE DESIGNER:**
Martha Baker Landscape Design

**CONTRACTOR:** Silva Building Contractors

## BEACHSIDE MODERN
page 56

**PROJECT TEAM:** Raymund Riparip, Andrew Wilson, Catherine Popple, Haley Burns

**INTERIOR DESIGNER:** Bella Mancini Design

**LANDSCAPE DESIGNER:** Gibney Design Landscape Architecture PC

**CONTRACTOR:** Schwantner & Sons Inc.

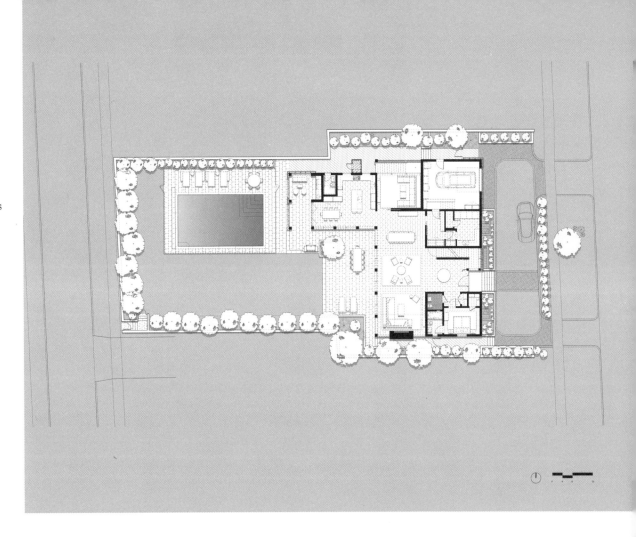

## A NEW LOOK
page 78

**PROJECT TEAM:** Christian Ricart, Ashley Walton, Julio Gavilanes, Karile Nefaite

**INTERIOR DESIGNER:** Fawn Galli Interior Design

**LANDSCAPE DESIGNER:** James Doyle Design Associates

**CONTRACTOR:** Brinton Brosius

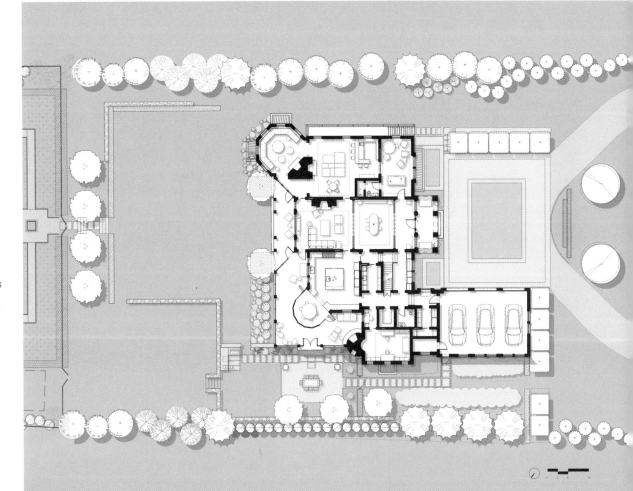

**BY THE BAY**
page 102

**PROJECT TEAM:**
Zach Ray, Julio Gavilanes

**INTERIOR DESIGNER:**
Bunny Williams Interior Design

**LANDSCAPE DESIGNER:**
LeBlanc Jones Landscape Architects

**CONTRACTOR:**
Silva Building Contractors

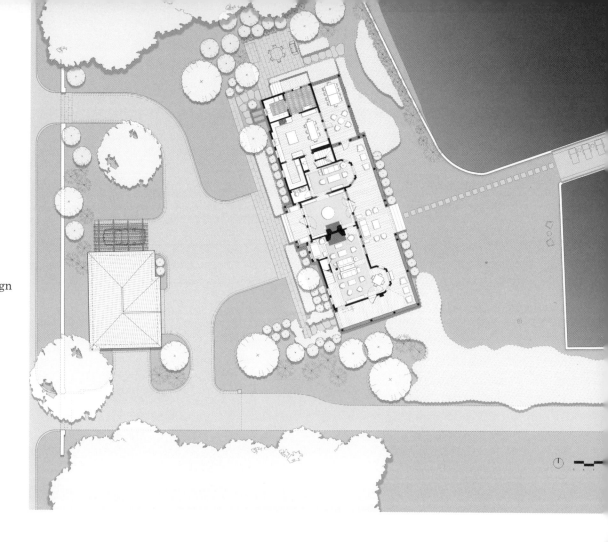

**RIVER'S EDGE**
page 122

**PROJECT TEAM:**
Zach Ray, Mariam Abdel Azim, Lauren Capps

**INTERIOR DESIGNER:**
Fawn Galli Interior Design

**LANDSCAPE DESIGNER:**
Michael Trapp

**CONTRACTOR:**
Charlton Construction

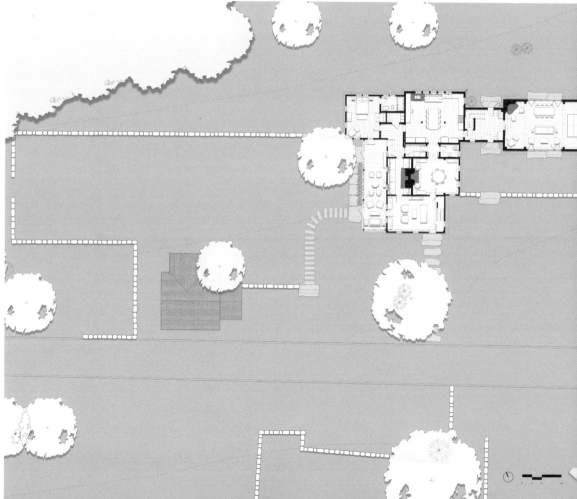

## SUBURBAN PAVILION
page 146

**PROJECT TEAM:**
Christian Ricart, Henry
Mulholland, Adam Welker

**INTERIOR DESIGNER:** LC Studio

**LANDSCAPE DESIGNER:**
Nievera Williams Design

**CONTRACTOR:** Quinndico

## FOREST TO FIELD
page 158

**PROJECT TEAM:**
Raymund Riparip, Hanna
Rutkouskaya, Gizem Bayhan,
Anahita Aliasgarian

**INTERIOR DESIGNER:**
Studio Magness, with additional
furniture and objects from
Foley & Cox HOME,
styled by Anita Sarsidi

**LANDSCAPE DESIGNER:**
James Doyle Design Associates

**CONTRACTOR:**
Pollack + Partners, LLC

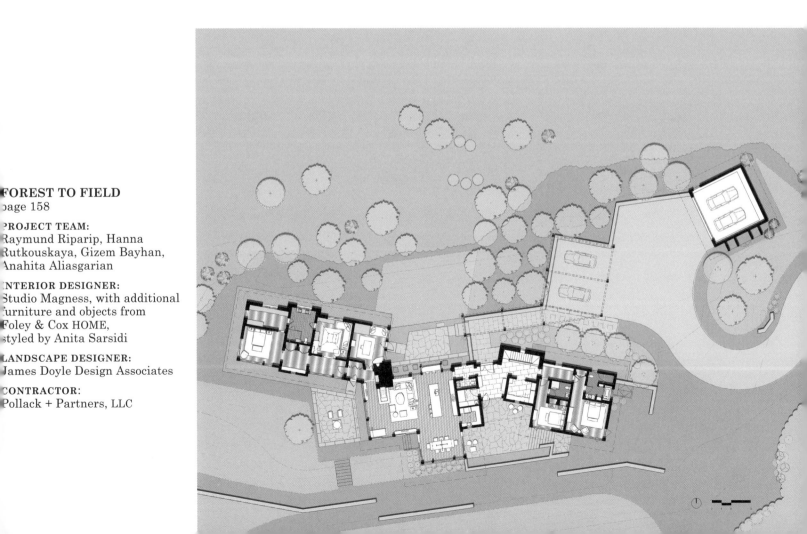

# ACKNOWLEDGMENTS

There are so many to thank while completing a first book. These brief words of acknowledgment are just as important as those that have come before.

Thank you to my representatives at the start of the process, Ellen Niven and Sydney Wallace, and those at Rizzoli who saw this book through to fruition, including publisher Charles Miers and editor Sandy Gilbert Freidus, designers Doug Turshen and David Huang, and writer Judith Nasatir.

Thank you to Bunny Williams and Brian McCarthy for generously sharing your ideas in the Foreword, the time you gave to bring it into being, and the projects we have collaborated on over the years, which have always opened my eyes to new possibilities.

I am grateful to my extraordinary clients whose vision, desire, and determination to build these homes and apartments inspire me endlessly. To the many talented interior designers, decorators, landscape designers, contractors, and artisans whose remarkable skills help transform our clients' lifestyles while at the same time enhancing my architecture, you have my deepest appreciation.

The images documented through the years by many superlative photographers make my architecture come alive in these pages. The architecture exists due to the unflagging efforts of my office, architects, bookkeepers, and support staff. You have my boundless thanks for your hard work and dedication. A special thanks to Andrew Wilson, Raymund Riparip, and Christian Ricart, who have been tireless project architects guiding the work over many years. Robert Miller, my deceased first partner, who helped get this all started, you have my sincerest appreciation. I wish you were here to participate in this publication.

Many friends have given generously of their time and offered much helpful insight over the years. Thank you all, especially Peter Hempel, Antonio Weiss, Rowan Gaither, my Yalies plus Roddy, the "gentlemen" of the Whisky Watercolor Club, Ankie Barnes, Michael Imber, Tom Kligerman, and Steve Rugo; to Sarah Magness in her own special place; to my parents and brother who provided a strong foundation; and finally to my children and their mother, Meredith, I see the world differently because of you.

To those of you mistakenly omitted, please accept my thanks, and my regrets.

Ravello is a place that lingers in one's dreams.

**PHOTOGRAPHY CREDITS**

Bjorn Wallander: pages 187, 200–201, 207–208, 211, 230–231, 233, 240–241

Costas Picada–Photos Dlux Creative: pages 124–125, 127–131, 133–139, 141–145

David Sundberg–Esto: pages 104–106, 108–109, 111–113, 115–121

Eric Piasecki Photography: pages 2, 10, 38, 40–42, 44–47, 49–55, 188–189, 203, 209, 218, 220–221

Francesco Lagnese Photography: pages 25–27, 29–35

Karen Fuchs: pages 4, 184–185, 191, 198–199, 210, 225–229, 239, 242–243

Mx Kim-Bee: pages 183, 196–197, 206, 216–217, 236–237

Richard Powers: pages 59–63, 65–69, 71–77, 80–81, 83–93, 95–99, 101, 148, 150–151, 153–157, 160, 162–165, 167–169, 171–173, 186, 192–193, 204–205, 213–215, 222–223, 238, 242–243, 257

Thomas Loof: pages 194–195, 219, 234–235

**INTERIOR DESIGNERS OF THE APARTMENTS**

Aman & Meeks Interior Design: pages 4, 184–185, 191, 198–199, 210, 225–229, 239, 242–243

Amy Lau Design: pages 194–195, 219, 234–235

Brian J. McCarthy: pages 183, 196–197, 206, 216–217, 236–237

Cullman & Kravis: pages 188–189, 203, 209, 218, 220–221

Fawn Galli Interior Design: pages 186, 192–193, 204–205, 213–215, 222–223, 238, 242–243

Foley & Cox Interiors: pages 187, 200–201, 207–208, 211, 230–231, 233, 240–241

**CONTRACTORS OF THE APARTMENTS**

Integkral Design Construction: pages 188–189, 203, 209, 218, 220–221

S Donadic Inc.: pages 187, 200–201, 207–208, 211, 230–231, 233, 240–241

Shay Construction: pages 183, 196–197, 206, 216–217, 236–237

SilverLining Inc.: pages 4, 184–185, 191, 194–195, 198–199, 210, 219, 225–229, 234–235, 239, 242–243

Zen Restoration: pages 186, 192–193, 204–205, 213–215, 222–223, 238, 242–243

First published in the United States of America in 2025 by
Rizzoli International Publications, Inc.
49 West 27th Street
New York, NY 10001
www.rizzoliusa.com

Copyright © 2025 Douglas Wright

All rights reserved. No part of this publication may be reproduced, stored in a retrieval system, or transmitted in any form or by any means, electronic, mechanical, photocopying, recording, or otherwise, without prior consent of the publishers.

Publisher: Charles Miers
Editor: Sandra Gilbert Freidus
Design: Doug Turshen with David Huang
Production Manager: Kaija Markoe
Editorial Coordination: Kelli Rae Patton and Sara Pozefsky
Managing Editor: Lynn Scrabis

ISBN: 978-0-8478-7431-6

Library of Congress Control Number: 2025935937

Printed in China
2025 2026 2027 2028 / 10 9 8 7 6 5 4 3 2 1

The authorized representative in the EU for product safety and compliance is Mondadori Libri S.p.A., via Gian Battista Vico 42, Milan, Italy, 20123, www.mondadori.it

Visit us online:
Instagram.com/RizzoliBooks
Facebook.com/RizzoliNewYork
Youtube.com/user/RizzoliNY

**Douglas Wright Architects** is a New York-based firm of architects and interior designers. Over the last fifteen years, it has designed award-winning projects nationwide, as well as in Europe, which have been featured in *Architectural Digest, Elle Decor, Veranda, Galerie,* and *The Wall Street Journal*. In 2023, the firm was honored with the Institute of Classical Architecture & Art's McKim, Mead & White award for residential architecture.

FRONT COVER: A New Jersey house moves the classic Shingle style into the twenty-first century.
BACK COVER, TOP, LEFT TO RIGHT: Baldassare Longhena's seventeenth-century Santa Maria della Salute; James Gibbs's eighteenth-century Radcliffe Camera at Oxford. CENTER, LEFT TO RIGHT: Favorite Italian memories include the Borghese Gardens in Rome; Ravello; and a palazzo terrace overlooking Siena. Bottom: Trajan's Forum in Rome. ENDPAPERS, FROM FRONT TO BACK: An afternoon on the Henry's Fork "Millionaires' Pond", Harriman Ranch, Idaho; concept sketches for a house in Maine; a classical temple atop the chimney of a suburban pool house pavilion; sunset over the Upper East Side of Manhattan.